What Every Husband Needs to Love His Wife
The Essentials and Rewards

Dr. Darrell D. Rose

Counseling and the Cross Publishers

Dedication

To my wife .wonderful wife Cynthia, for your exceptional support in making me the Godly man that I am today.

To my Sons, Aaron and Jonathan, to help you become the best Christ-Like husband that God would have you to be.

Contents

Foreword

L oving your wife isn't just a command—it's your calling. From the very beginning, God designed marriage to be a living testimony of His love, faithfulness, and grace. When husbands love their wives as Christ loves the Church, they not only bless their homes but also bear witness to the power of the gospel in everyday life. That is why the message of this book is so vital and so timely.

In What Every Husband Needs to Love His Wife: The Essentials and Rewards, Dr. Darrell D. Rose gives husbands a gift—biblical wisdom wrapped in practical guidance, written with the heart of a pastor and the clarity of a teacher. He speaks directly to men in a way that is honest, convicting, and full of hope. He doesn't sugarcoat the challenges of marriage, but he also never leaves the reader without the encouragement and tools needed to grow.

In the first part of the book, Dr. Rose highlights the essentials every husband must embrace: wisdom and understanding, sacrificial giving, humility, patience, gentleness, and a reliance on God. These are not just traits to admire; they are practices to live out daily. In the second part, he points us toward the rewards that follow when we love God's way—deeper intimacy with Christ, personal growth and peace, and the joy of true connection with our wives.

What I appreciate most is that this book does not place the burden of perfection on a husband's shoulders. Instead, it calls us to depend on God's strength, reminding us that loving well begins not with trying harder, but with drawing nearer to Christ. That perspective alone can transform not only marriages but lives.

Whether you are a newlywed or have been married for many years, this book will inspire you, challenge you, and encourage you to keep loving faithfully. It will help you see your wife not as a responsibility to manage but as a treasure to cherish. And it will remind you that when you love your wife God's way, your home becomes a reflection of Christ's love for His Church.

On a personal note, I wish to commend Dr. Rose for authoring this work with remarkable depth, clarity, and compassion. For more than two decades, Dr. Rose and his wife, Cynthia, have faithfully served the congregation of Good Hope Missionary Baptist Church in Houston, Texas, where I have had the honor of serving as senior pastor since 1994. Drawing upon his extensive experience in biblical counseling, Dr. Rose offers keen insights into some of the most pressing and complex challenges faced in marriage. To speak into the hearts of men requires both courage and humility, and he demonstrates each with unwavering conviction and grace. I am profoundly grateful for his obedience to God's call in undertaking this work, and I am confident it will edify and strengthen marriages for generations to come.

My prayer is that every husband who reads this book will find fresh vision, renewed passion, and lasting joy in his marriage. May you take these truths to heart, apply them with humility, and experience the rich blessings God has promised to those who love in His way.

Practical. Biblical. Transformative. This book will help you become the husband God designed you to be.

—Dr. D. Z. Cofield, Senior Pastor, Good Hope Missionary Baptist Church,

Houston

Introduction

When you pick up a can of Campbell's Chicken Noodle Soup, the label tells you everything you need to know: the ingredients, the nutritional value, and the preparation instructions. As a retired Executive Hotel Chef, I've always paid close attention to labels—because what goes inside matters. By-products, fillers, and cheap substitutes may look the part, but they never provide the nourishment we need.

Love is no different. Many husbands think they are showing love when in reality, they are offering cheap substitutes. Words without actions, manipulation to get what they want, or equating financial provision with affection are nothing more than by-products of a worldly definition of love. They may look like love, but they cannot nourish a marriage. They leave a wife unsatisfied, and a husband unfulfilled.

The Bible gives us the true "ingredients" in 1 Corinthians 13:4–8: patience, kindness, humility, gentleness, forgiveness, endurance, hope, and faithfulness. These are not fillers. They are the essentials that make love authentic and life-giving. And just like a recipe, the order and balance matter. Remove one ingredient, and the love is incomplete.

But here's the truth every husband must face: you cannot love your wife like this on your own. You may have moments of patience, flashes of kindness, or occasional humility, but to love consistently as Christ loves requires something greater than human strength. It requires wisdom, understanding, sacrifice, and the power of the Holy Spirit working through you. That's why this book is not just about principles—it's about transformation.

In **Section One**, we will look closely at the essentials of love:

- **Wisdom and Understanding** – knowing God, yourself, and your wife.

- **Sacrifice through Giving** – because true love costs something.

- **Humility** – setting aside pride to serve your wife.

- **Gentleness and Mercy** – offering compassion even when she falls short.

- **Patience and Longsuffering** – enduring with love, even in hard seasons.

- **Divine Intervention** – relying on Christ through the Spirit for the strength you do not have on your own.

Each of these essentials is like a key ingredient in God's recipe for a thriving marriage.

In **Section Two**, we will discover the rewards of loving your wife God's way:

- **Spiritual Rewards** – deeper fellowship with God, His favor, answered prayer, and His blessings on your life.

- **Personal Rewards** – a peaceful heart, a fruitful home, and resilience to withstand life's storms.

- **Relational Rewards** – peace with your wife, forgiveness, intimacy, companionship, and the joy of growing old together.

These rewards are not shallow perks; they are life-transforming blessings. A husband who loves his wife biblically not only strengthens his marriage but also testifies to the power of Christ in his home. His love becomes a witness to his children, his community, and even the world.

So I invite you, as you read these pages, to ask yourself: *What ingredients am I bringing into my marriage? Have I been offering my wife the fullness of Christ's love, or have I been substituting love with worldly fillers?*

The good news is that no matter where you are today, God can supply what is missing. Through His Word and by His Spirit, you can learn to love your wife in a way that brings her joy, glorifies God, and fills your own life with peace and blessing.

Just as a hot bowl of Campbell's Chicken Noodle Soup warms the body, so Christlike love—authentic, nourishing, and enduring—will result in divine rewards that will warm your marriage and make it thrive.

PART ONE: THE ESSENTIALS FOR LOVING YOUR WIFE

Acquiring the Necessary tools that will help Husbands Love Their Wives

Chapter 1

Loving Your Wife Like Christ Requires Wisdom and Understanding

George and Nancy

I once encountered a couple in desperate need of counseling. Let's call this couple Dr. George and Nancy to protect the couple's identity. George had a Ph.D. in medicine and worked as a professor at a prestigious Medical College in Houston. His wife, Nancy, worked as a CPA and investment broker. Nancy reached out to me for marriage counseling. So, I sent her and George a Personal Data Inventory form (PDI) to complete as a prerequisite for all counseling requests. Nancy completed and submitted the PDI to our counseling administrator on the same day she received it, but George submitted his completed PDI three weeks later.

In the first session, we introduced ourselves and became acquainted. Afterward, I began asking intensive questions to understand their marriage problem based on their perspective. During the later part of the session, I asked each of them what are problem(s) in their marriage are, as they see it.

George yelled, "I do not see where the problem is! Everything is fine in our marriage. I am not even sure why she is so adamant about coming to counseling."

Nancy responded, "And that's the problem! George is so caught up with his job that he is disconnected from our relationship. He is arrogant and denounces me as a person. George does not respect me. He wants to control everything, and whatever he says goes. The reason why he submitted his PDI late is that he did not want to come to counseling. He said he did not need another man telling him how to run his house and marriage."

So, I asked George if what Nancy just shared was true. He denied everything Nancy said, except the latter, which Nancy stated was his reason for not wanting to come to counseling. At this time, I assured them that I cared about what they were going through and offered hope and encouragement. To give George and Nancy hope, I pointed them to First Corinthians 10:13 to show that the problems they are experiencing are not unique and are common in marriages. I reminded them that God's Word has answers to their problems.

Then, we discussed the parable in Matthew 7:24-27, where Jesus compares the wise man to a foolish man. Jesus says the man who hears and obeys his words is like a wise man who builds his house on a rock and endures the storm. But the man who hears Jesus' words but does not obey is like a foolish man who built his house on sand, and when the storm came, the house collapsed because it was built on a poor foundation. After reading and explaining the parable, I asked them to consider their marriage a house.

Then I asked, "In the storms you are now experiencing, would you say your marriage relationship is still standing, or has it fallen? Have you built your marriage on the rock, obedience to the Word of God, or sand?"

Nancy said, "It has fallen because it was not built on the Word of God."

George refuted her answer, saying, "I disagree. I believe it is still standing."

Then it happened. George said something that took the wind out of the room. He accused me of misusing Matthew 7:24-27 without providing a definitive reason.

Then he asked, "How many sessions are you planning to have with us?"

I told him, "It would probably be roughly eight to twelve sessions."

George said, "Oh, I thought we were meeting for one session. This session will be our first and our last. Thank you for your time."

A few weeks later, I spoke with Nancy in passing at church and asked how things were going. With tear-filled eyes, she said, "pastor, please pray for us."

Of course, whenever there are problems in a marriage, both husband and wife are at fault to some degree. But in the case of George and Nancy, what was George's problem? The problem stems from his view and understanding of God, himself, and his wife. George had a distorted view of God. As a result of having a deflated view of God, George instinctively had an inflated view of himself.

Moreover, George mistakenly equated secular education, personal accomplishments, gifts, and talents with wisdom. His inflated view of himself compelled him to view his wife as an object to be used and controlled rather than a woman to be loved as Christ loved the church. He failed to fulfill his biblical role as a husband because he lacked wisdom and understanding of God and himself and failed to live with his wife in an understanding way.

In this chapter, I intend to show you that loving your wife like Christ requires wisdom and understanding of God, yourself, and your wife.

Wisdom and Understanding of God is Essential to Loving Your Wife

Wisdom and understanding of God are essential elements for loving your wife biblically. As I stated earlier, the main ingredients on the nutrient labels of food packages are listed first. Why are wisdom and understanding the first and primary ingredients for loving your wife and being the Christ-like husband God calls you to be? They are listed first because the measure of a godly man, a spiritually mature husband, is not based on your maleness and masculinity, as the world suggests. The measure of a spiritually mature man/husband is wisdom and understanding of the person of God. The apostle James wrote about the measure of one's spiritual maturity. He said,

Who among you is wise and understanding? Let him show by his good behavior his deeds in the gentleness of wisdom. (James 3:13)

James says if anyone claims to be wise and understanding, he needs to show it by his behavior. Talk is cheap. But what does James mean by "wise" and "understanding?" I have used James 3:13 on several occasions in marriage counseling and teaching. When I ask couples what does James mean by the phrase "wise and understanding," I receive a variety of responses. Here are a few common responses. Some will say to be "Wise and understanding" means to be experienced in dealing with life problems." Others have said, "To be wise and understanding means to be able to make good decisions that are in the family's best interest." A few men have said, "To be wise and understanding means to effectively provide for, protect, lead, and guide your wife and children." These are all reasonable responses but these definitions are primarily rooted in a worldly perspective. How do we know? Because, in each of these common responses, God is not the focal point.

So, what does James mean by "wise" and "understanding?" Let's consider what the Bible says about these terms. Proverbs 1:7 says,

The fear of the Lord is the beginning of knowledge; Fools despise wisdom and instruction.

The word "fear" in this text means to be in awe of or to revere God, which makes one receptive to wisdom and knowledge; it means knowing God experientially. From a biblical perspective, the source of knowledge is the fear of the Lord. To further unpack the meaning of "wise" and "understanding," let's consider the Book of Job. In response to Job's questions to God concerning the suffering Job was experiencing, God asks Job the following rhetorical question:

"But where can wisdom be found? And where is the place of understanding? (Job 28:12).

After God asks Job the rhetorical question, God provides the answer. First, God tells Job where wisdom and understanding cannot be found. God said that man cannot discover it or find divine wisdom and knowledge in the things of this world (Job 28:13-22). God says, "But I know where they can found," because wisdom and understanding come from me (Job 28:23-27). Finally, God gives a punchline answer to where wisdom and understanding can be found. God said to Job,

"And to man, He said, 'Behold, the fear of the Lord, that is wisdom; And to depart from evil is understanding.'" (Job 28:28).

God says to be wise is to reverence, worship, and submit to his authority, and understanding is to avoid evil by walking in obedience to His Word. So, what does being wise and understanding have to do with being a spiritually mature husband and loving your wife? The Apostle James says it is the proof of your spiritual maturity. Wisdom and understanding have everything to do with being the husband God has called you to be and your ability to love your wife as Christ loved the church. Let's revisit James 3:13. James asked and then he answers his own question. He says,

Who among you is wise and understanding? Let him show by his good behavior his deeds in the gentleness of wisdom. (James 3:13)

A proper view and response to God are evidence of being a godly man and a spiritually mature husband. But who is God, and what is it about him that you need to embrace? Although it is not an exhaustive list, here are a few examples of the attributes of God every husband should embrace. First, God is Sovereign – he is first, and above all things, he can do whatever he chooses, and no one can change what he has done (Eccl. 7:13-14) Second, God is the Supreme authority – He is the supreme ruler over heaven and the earth and is subject only to himself (1 Chron. 29:11-12) Third, God is holy – excellent in every way and the epitome of moral perfection (1 Jn. 1:5) Fourth, God is faithful – He is an unwavering God who always keeps his promises (Lam. 3:22-23). Fifth, God is gracious and merciful – he gives unmerited favor to the unworthy and pardons those who deserve punishment (Ps. 145:9; Eph. 2:8-9). Of course, there are many rich attributes of God that husbands need to embrace, which I did not mention because they would go beyond the scope of this chapter. But the point is that having a proper view of God is essential to loving your wife. Knowledge of who God is alone is not enough if we do not embrace what we know about God as truth. Knowing and embracing the God of the Bible requires a proper response of reverence, worship, submission, and thanksgiving (Rom. 1:21). What is the evidence or proof that you have a proper view of God? The proof is how well you relate to others, particularly your wife.

James says the proof is your good deeds (actions) performed in a spirit of gentleness (attitude). The word "gentleness" in this text refers humility that results from knowing and embracing the character of God, which compels us to relate to others with gentleness. The evidence of your love for your wife is not based on how often you tell her you love her, but your love for your wife equals your level of wisdom and understanding of God. The evidence of knowledge and understanding of God is demonstrated by how well you relate to your wife in a spirit of humility and gentleness. The wisdom and understanding that comes down from above will help cultivate love and unity with your wife and maintain order in your home.

But James warns us about another source of wisdom and understanding, which you must be aware of and avoid. The second source of wisdom and understanding that James speaks of is an enemy to you, your wife, and your marriage. After discussing the evidence of one who has Godly wisdom and understanding, James goes on to say,

But if you have bitter jealousy and selfish ambition in your heart, do not be arrogant and so lie against the truth. This wisdom is not that which comes down from above, but is earthly, natural, demonic For where jealousy and selfish ambition exist, there is disorder and every evil thing (James 3:14-16)

Here, James is describing the wisdom and understanding that comes from the world, the flesh, and Satan. If you demand that your wife give you what you want, and become angry at her because she is not giving it. If what you are demanding from her is for your benefit and not hers, then you are operating according to worldly, fleshly, and demonic wisdom. Suppose your wife confronts you with the truth about your pride and selfishness, and you pretend that you are attempting to do what is best for the relationship when your true motive is personal gain. In verse 3:15, James says that this kind of behavior is not that which comes down from above, but it is the kind that comes up from below. In other words, this wisdom is rooted in human nature (the natural inclinations of the sinful heart/flesh), earthly (like those of the world), and demonic (satanically influenced).

What is the evidence of Godly wisdom and understanding compared to worldly wisdom and understanding? I've already stated that the evidence of Godly wisdom is humility, gentleness, love, unity, and order in your relationship with your wife. On the other hand, James says that "disorder, and every evil thing" is the evidence of one who is walking according to the wisdom and understanding of the world.

What does disorder and every evil thing look like in a marriage? Here are a few examples of disorder in a marriage:

1. Role reversals – a wife who is leading and her husband is following

2. War between husband and wife

3. Ongoing battles and flair-ups

4. Division in the marital relationship

5. Blow up mudslinging arguments

6. Kids/Teenagers are out of control because of the lack of discipline

7. Stonewalling – shutting down and refusing to talk

8. Neglect and lack of intimacy or physical touch

Not only is "disorder" in the marriage a sign of operation according to the wisdom and understanding of the world, but James says that "every evil thing" is the other side of the same coin. What does "every evil thing" look like in a marriage? Consider the following examples of evil: Anger, bitterness, resentment, manipulation, cursing, plotting, scheming, disunity, unforgiveness, slander, hatred, physical and verbal abuse, sexual immorality, impurity, and murder. You may say that "Murder is extreme. I may be guilty of committing some of these evil things, but I would never murder my wife." Murder is indeed extreme, but Jesus says if you are angry with and refer to your brother or sister as a "good for nothing" or "fool," then you are guilty of murder (Matt. 5:21-23). In other words, if you become so angry with your wife that you ascribe to her a derogatory name or title in your heart, even if unspoken, then you are guilty of murder. These characteristics are the opposite of loving your wife as Christ loved the church.

On the other hand, James says that the wisdom from God is the extreme opposite of the wisdom from the world. The following is what James wrote about characteristics of Godly wisdom. James says,

But the wisdom from above is first pure, then peaceable, gentle, reasonable, full of mercy and good fruits, unwavering, without hypocrisy. And the seed whose fruit is righteousness is sown in peace by those who make peace. (James 3:17-18)

In summary, wisdom and understanding of God are essential foundational elements for loving your wife biblically. As I stated, the measure of a godly man, a spiritually mature husband, is not based on your maleness and masculinity, as the world suggests. The measure of a spiritually mature man/husband is wisdom and understanding of the person of God. Wisdom and understanding will help you cultivate love and unity with your wife and maintain order in your home. Most of all, it will establish peace from God, and that peace will infiltrate between you and your wife.

If you are going to love your wife, you must be aware of and guard against operating according to your flesh and the wisdom of the world. The degree to which you demonstrate love for your wife is equivalent to the degree to which you love God. A proper view of God will compel you to love your wife and help you acquire a proper view of self, which is the next important part of wisdom and understanding essential to loving your wife.

Understanding Yourself is Essential to Loving Your Wife

Understanding yourself is essential to loving your wife. Wisdom and understanding of God will give you a proper view of yourself. You were made in God's image, created to be a dependent worshipper, born as an enemy of God, rescued from the penalty of sin and death, and exist for God's glory.

First, we were made in the image of God. To be created in the image of God means that you possess, in a limited sense, some of God's attributes, referred to as God's communicable attributes. In other words, attributes such as rational thought, emotional capacity, volitional freedom, spiritual life, moral and ethical sensitivities, and conscience are all communicable attributes of God that He shares with us. On the other hand, man does not possess God's non-communicable attributes. We are not omnipotent, omniscient, or omnipresent; these are non-communicable attributes that belong only to God.

Second, we were created to be dependent worshippers. We must depend upon God for vertical and horizontal companionship. Genesis 2:18 says, the LORD God said, "It is not good for the man to be alone; I will make him a helper suitable for him." But, before creating Eve in Genesis 2:21, God brought the animals before Adam to have him name the animals (Gen. 2:19-20). Ironically, God said it was not good for Adam to be alone, but before creating Eve, he had Adam name the animals first. Why? It appears that God wanted Adam to know that he (Adam) lacked something and what Adam needed Adam could not provide independently of God. What does Adam's story have to do with us husbands? We were created to be dependent worshippers of God because we need someone more prominent and more powerful than we are to provide what we cannot provide for ourselves. We cannot be the husbands God calls us to be apart from divine intervention. Throughout Scripture, man has always depended on God to rescue him from unfavorable situations, circumstances, and events.

But be mindful that unfavorable situations, circumstances, and events are external temptations, trials, and tests that occur outside of us and are out of our control. But we also need God to rescue us from ourselves. The sinful inclinations of the flesh, are internal temptations, happen in the inside of us and, if we yield to them, cause us to be self-destructive. Sinful desires, thoughts, and attitudes are characteristics of the flesh that reside in our hearts (Jer. 17:9). Jesus said,

For from within, out of the heart of men, proceed the evil thoughts, fornications, thefts, murders, adulteries, deeds of coveting and wickedness, as well as deceit, sensuality, envy, slander, pride and foolishness. All these evil things proceed from within and defile the man." (Mark 7:21-23)

We must depend on God to provide us with the divine strength to suppress the sinful inclination of our hearts (our flesh). As a prison guard, surveillance, and keeping prisoners in check, so must we as husbands guard our hearts and keep sinful desires and thoughts incarcerated (Pr. 4:23). Guarding your heart is essential to loving your wife. But mere willpower does not work in combating the flesh. If we are going to love our wives, as God commands, we need the power of the Holy Spirit (to be discussed later in chapter 6). We must depend on God.

Third, we are imperfect beings, born as enemies of God. But by the grace of God, we have been rescued from the penalty of sin and death. Scripture says we are naturally born sinners since our mother's wound (Ps. 51:5). And any righteousness we try to produce while walking in sin is as filthy rags before God (Isa. 64:6). We all fall short of the glory of God (Rom. 3:23). Moreover, we are instinctively enemies of God by nature, dead in our sins, practiced habitual disobedience, and lived our lives according to the ways of the world, indulging in the desires of our sinful flesh (Eph. 2:1-3).

But by God's grace, Christ delivered us from the penalty of sin and death (Eph. 2:4-9). Against the backdrop of what the Bible says about our nature, we, as husbands, should never think more highly of ourselves than we ought to think (Rom. 12:3). We are not all that and a bag of chips. We are imperfect men who miss the mark at times. But glory to God for his grace and mercy upon us.

Last, we exist to glorify God but we cannot glorify God as the Creator apart from Jesus Christ (2 Cor. 5:9). We can only glorify God by conforming to the likeness of His Son (Rom. 8:28-29). A proper view of God compels us to have a proper view of ourselves. A proper view of self produces righteous behaviors of humility and gentleness, driven by loving attitudes and demonstrated actions that glorify God because they reflect the image of Christ.

Conversely, if your view of God is deflated, you will instinctively have an inflated view of yourself. In other words, some of those with a deflated view of God tend to love themselves more than they love God and others, which violates Jesus' command to love God and others (Matt.22:37-39).

How does this mindset show up in a marriage regarding how a husband relates to his wife? A husband who loves himself will have an exaggerated and inflated view of his self-worth and self-importance, have an excessive desire for admiration, a sense of entitlement, expect to be catered to and served by his wife, commit interpersonal exploitation, and view himself as superior to his wife.

I have counseled husbands who came for marriage counseling and exhibited this type of behavior. I lovingly try to help them realize that God holds the husband more responsible for the marriage than the wife because the husband is the head. Some of them rejected my counsel. But here is a warning. A husband who refuses to take responsibility for the marriage and relates to his wife in an unloving way will forfeit his blessing. God will not answer his prayers (Jn. 9:31). Therefore, I encourage you to maintain the right perspective of God and a proper view of self that aligns with God's Word. Seeing yourself as God sees you is essential to loving your wife. Not only do you need an understanding of God and yourself. But you also need to understand your wife.

Understanding Your Wife Is Essential to Loving Her

Understanding your wife is essential to loving her. I have counseled many married couples over the last two decades. During our introduction in the first session, I usually ask questions to understand the context of their situation. After exchanging pleasantries and becoming acquainted, I will ask them to share their individual perspectives on their marriage's problem(s). As I did with George and Nancy, I will ask, "What is the problem in your marriage as you see it?"

In most cases, each spouse can articulate what they believe is the problem in their marriage. Married couples often enter the first counseling session, pointing their figure at one another as if the other person is solely the cause of their problems. Finger-pointing is not unusual in marriage counseling because Scripture says all a man's ways are right in his own eyes, but God weighs the heart (Ps. 16:2). However, on a few occasions, a wife has shared her perspective of the source of the problem in the marriage and her husband appears to be oblivious to the issues. Here are familiar statements from husbands oblivious to the problems in their marriages: "We have a good marriage; I don't see where the problem is." These statements are indicative of a problem in and of themselves. Why? These statements indicate a husband who has failed to live with his wife in an understanding way. They are living with their wives, but they do not know them. Sure, there may be times when a wife may not share her concerns or when something is bothering her. But even in times like these, a husband should be so spiritually and emotionally in tune with his wife that he can sense something is wrong even though she has not said a word. The same goes for wives in their connection with their husbands. Any husband and wife who have been married for a while can attest to this truth.

Apostle Peter emphasizes this principle when he said,

You husbands, in the same way, live with your wives in an understanding way, as with someone weaker, since she is a woman, and show her honor as a fellow heir of the grace of life so that your prayers will not be hindered. (1 Pet. 3:7)

Let's examine this verse in more detail. Peter begins this verse by saying, "You husbands in the same way." But what does Peter mean by "In the same way?" The phrase, "In the same way," shows up the first time when he addresses wives' submission to their husbands in 1 Peter 3:1. So we need to go back to what Peter said earlier in chapter 2 to understand what he means. In chapter 2, Peter talks about submission to those in authority, not only to those who are good but to those who are harsh, cruel, or unreasonable (1 Pet. 2:18). Then Peter states if a man endures suffering unjustly because of his commitment to the Lord, he will find God's favor (1 Pet. 2:19-20). Finally, he says Jesus is the role model we should follow when encountering unjust suffering (1 Pet. 2:21-24).

Now that the context of First Peter 3:7 has been established, let's return to the original question. In the backdrop of 1 Peter 2:18-24, what does Peter mean by saying, "You husbands in the same way?" Based on 1 Peter 2:18-24, it means that husbands should live with their wives in an understanding way even if they have to suffer unjustly. Why should we do it? Peter says,

For this *finds* favor, if for the sake of conscience toward God a person bears up under sorrows when suffering unjustly (1 Pet. 2:19).

It finds favor with God. How do you find favor with God? You find favor with God when you are mindful of God's command to love your wife as Christ loved the church and commit to fulfilling your biblical role as husband, even if it requires you to endure unjust suffering. Additionally, Peter says, "No matter how difficult the task is, live with your wife in an understanding way."

But how can you acquire an accurate understanding of your wife? If you are going to love and understand your wife, then you must study her. Most college students know that to do well on an exam, they must study by reviewing the assigned reading materials and notes taken during the lectures. Students who fail to take notes during class will have difficulty passing the exam. What does studying for an exam have to do with understanding your wife? Understanding your wife requires you to study her and take notes. Taking notes about your wife does not necessarily require a pen and paper, but mental notes would suffice. You need to know your wife physically, emotionally, spiritually, and mentally. You need to know her strengths, weaknesses, fears, likes, and dislikes.

For example, during marriage counseling sessions, I will sometimes ask the husband a few questions to test how well he knows his wife. I may ask, "Do you understand and know your wife?" Most husbands answer with a resounding "Yes." So, I take it a step further by asking a string of intensive questions such as: "Okay. What is her favorite color, restaurant, TV show, and movie? What are her fears and concerns? What makes her unique? What would she likely order from the menu if you all went to your favorite restaurant? What is the name of the perfume she wears, the soap she uses, and the scent?" As the husband often attempts to answer these questions, he glances at his wife to confirm his answers are correct. Some wives will have bright smiles, with their eyes fixated on their husbands. If the husband answers most of the questions correctly, he is commended by me as the counselor and praised by his wife. Most husbands are delighted when they receive praise from their wives. Why? Because many of us desire affirmation from our wives. But on the other hand, some husbands answered these questions incorrectly and received opposite responses from their wives. Instead of receiving a bright smile of praise from their wives, these men see disappointment and sadness in their wives' facial expressions. What is the point?

The point is that knowing your wife requires that you study and take notes. Knowing your wife requires that you observe her like a CSI investigator, paying attention to meticulous details about the way she thinks, behavior patterns, emotions, needs, and desires. You need to know her likes and dislikes. You also need to know your wife's body and where every pimple is located. You need to know how she likes to be touched and where. When you strive to understand your wife on every level, it will make her feel valued and loved. She will praise you for living with her in an understanding way.

Understanding Your Wife Compels You to Handle Her with Care

Not only must you live with her in an understanding way, but you must also be mindful that she is the weaker vessel. Remember, Peter wrote, "You husbands, in the same way, live with your wives in an understanding way, **as with someone weaker, since she is a woman...**" (1 Pet 3:7). It is a given that men are generally physically stronger than women. Men were divinely created for physical work. However, Peter's word "weaker" in this passage does not necessarily refer to physical strength. Being weaker does not mean that your wife is less than or inferior. Being weaker does not mean her gifts, abilities, and talents are less valuable and less important than yours. Weaker, simply put, means that your wife is like crystal glass or fine China, and you must handle her with care because she is easily broken. The post office attendees who accept packages for shipping have a stamp that reads, "Fragile; Handle with care" that they stamp on all packages containing glass or delicate items. So it is with your wife. You love your wife when you understand that she is a weaker vessel, and you handle her with gentleness and care because she is easily broken.

Conclusion

Wisdom and understanding of God are essential elements for loving your wife biblically. The measure of a godly husband is wisdom and understanding of the person of God and what he commands of you as a husband, an understanding of yourself through the lens of Scripture, and an understanding of your wife. A proper view and response to God is foundational to being a godly and spiritually mature husband. The proof of your love for your wife is not based on how often you tell her you love her. But your love for your wife begins with the degree of your wisdom and understanding of God. The evidence of wisdom and understanding of God is demonstrated by how well you relate to your wife in a spirit of humility and gentleness.

Moreover, understanding yourself is essential to loving your wife. A proper view of God will compel you to have an appropriate view of yourself. Last, understanding your wife is essential to loving her. As I stated earlier, you will find favor with God when you are mindful of God's command to love your wife as Christ loved the church. God expects you to commit to fulfilling your biblical role as husband, even if it requires you to endure unjust suffering. When you strive to understand your wife on every level, it will make her feel valued and loved. More importantly, you will find favor with God. Not only are wisdom and understanding essential to loving your wife, but sacrifice through giving is also essential to loving your wife, as you will see in the next chapter.

Reflection Questions

1. In what ways have you relied on worldly wisdom (career success, pride, control) instead of godly wisdom in your marriage?

2. How well do you truly know your wife — her fears, desires, joys, and struggles? What specific steps could you take this week to better understand her?

3. What daily practice could you begin that would help you keep a right view of God, a humble view of yourself, and an honoring view of your wife?

Chapter 2

Loving Your Wife as Christ Loved the Church requires Sacrificial Giving.

Caleb and Catherine

The movie Fireproof tells the story of a couple whose marriage is on the brink of divorce. Caleb is a firefighter captain, and his wife, Catherine, works at a hospital. Their marriage is in trouble. Caleb makes one last dire effort to save his marriage and keep it from going up in flames. Unbeknownst to his wife, he withdrew $24,000 from his savings account (funds he saved to purchase his dream boat) and donated it towards buying a hospital bed for his wife's elderly and sick mother. Catherine assumed that the large donation the hospital bed supply company received to purchase her mother's bed was the result of a generous contribution from an overly friendly doctor she worked with. However, during a conversation with a hospital supply sales representative, Catherine quickly discovered that the doctor only contributed $300, and the remaining $24,000 came from her husband, Caleb. Out of humility, Caleb did not previously disclose to Catherine the magnitude of his willingness to sacrifice and give to save his marriage. The movie ends with Caleb and Catherine embracing each other with tear-filled eyes on their way to reuniting and restoring their marriage. Even though it was just a movie, Fireproof depicts how a husband should love his wife through sacrifice and giving. The theme of this movie was a motto adopted by firefighters that says, "Never leave your partner behind."

Do you love your wife? If so, what sacrifices are you willing to make for her? What would you give up to strengthen your marriage? If your relationship were on the brink of collapse, like Caleb, would you be willing to lay aside your desires, your comfort, even your dreams to fight for your marriage?

This chapter explores how sacrificial giving creates opportunities for oneness, restoration, healing, and reconciliation. The aim is to show how loving your wife requires sacrificial giving.

What is True Sacrifice?

What is the meaning of "sacrifice?" Merriam-Webster's Dictionary defines sacrifice as "an act of offering to a deity something precious" or "a destruction or surrender of something for the sake of something else." Another dictionary defines sacrifice as "the surrender or destruction of something prized or desirable for the sake of something considered as having a higher or more pressing claim" (or favorable outcome). [1] The word "sacrifice" is also used among baseball fans and players. In baseball, a "sacrifice fly" occurs when a player deliberately hits a pitched baseball deep into the outfield to be caught by an outfielder of the opposing team, advancing a runner to home plate to score a run.

But what is the biblical meaning of "sacrifice?" According to the Oxford Dictionary of the Christian Church, "Sacrifice is fundamentally the offering to the Deity as a gift, esp. a living creature."[2] In the Old Testament, offering animals and plant foods as gifts to God was an act of worship. Presenting sacrifices to God also emphasized giving something of value. Sacrifices were also for the atonement of sins, of the community of God's people, and of individual members of the faith. In the Bible, atonement refers to the unity and harmony between God and humanity. Sin creates a division between God and man. Since the penalty for sin is death, animal sacrifices were presented to God to atone for sin and to reconcile the relationship and fellowship between God and sinners (Gen. 4:2-4, 8:20; Ex. 12:1-30). But sacrifice is impossible without giving.

What is Giving?

How would you define "giving?" Most of us know that the general meaning of "giving" is to make a voluntary donation or gift to another, expecting nothing in return. But what comes to mind for most people when they think of giving is money. The probable reason why most people think of money when it comes to giving is that money is considered a valuable asset or commodity.

But there are certain types of gifts that money cannot buy. In the New Testament, Jesus Christ is the sacrificial Lamb who gave his life as the propitiation (payment) for the sins of the world (Rom. 3:25, 5:11, 19, 6:23). Matthew 20:28 says, "just as the Son of Man did not come to be served, but to serve, and to give his life as a ransom for many."

In Matthew 20:28, "give" is the Greek word "dounai," which means to die for, lay down one's life, or to give or deliver oneself over to death on behalf of another. Jesus Christ sacrificed his life by giving up his life for the sins of the world. Scripture also says, "For God so loved the world, that He gave His only begotten Son, that whoever believes in Him shall not perish, but have eternal life" (John 3:16).

Here again, God demonstrated love by sacrificing his son for the present and eternal benefits of those who believe. What is interesting about Matthew 20:28 and John 3:16 is that both show that the love of God is demonstrated by sacrifice through the giving of something invaluable for the benefit of another. In essence, a person's love for another can be measured by how much they are willing to sacrifice and the value of the gift they are willing to give for the benefit of another. For instance, we have all received and exchanged gifts with family and friends on Christmas Day. A common motto held by some is, "It is not about the gift; it's the thought that counts." I am sure you may have received a gift from someone, and after opening it, you thought, "Well, it wasn't much thought put into this one." Some people will present gifts that do not fit their preference as "regifts" to others. The point is that the value of the gift to the giver is equal to the magnitude of the sacrifice. If a person claims to love another, yet the value of the gift he is willing to sacrifice has no value, it cannot always be viewed as a true sacrifice. Sacrifices occur when you give up something that you deem valuable for the benefit of another.

Sacrificial Giving in Marriage

Now that we have defined "sacrifice" and "giving," how do they relate, and how does this translate to loving your wife as Christ loved the church? Ephesians 5:25-27 says,

> "Husbands, love your wives, just as Christ also loved the church and gave Himself up for her, so that He might sanctify her, having cleansed her by the washing of water with the word, that He might present to Himself the church in all her glory, having no spot or wrinkle or any such thing; but that she would be holy and blameless."

Scripture commands that a husband love his wife as Christ loved the church by giving himself as a living sacrifice. In essence, a husband must die to himself, his desires, affections, and self-interests. What keeps us from making sacrifices and giving ourselves up for our wives? The answer is selfishness and vain glory. Philippians 2:3-4 says,

> Do nothing from selfishness or empty conceit, but with humility of mind, regard one another as more important than yourselves; do not merely look out for your own personal interests, but also for the interests of others.

Some of your desires, affections, and personal interests are neutral; they are neither wrong nor right according to Scripture. However, your desires, affections, and personal interests can become sinful when you prioritize them more than your wife, if you seek to hold on to them tightly and refuse to sacrifice them for your wife's benefit. Being overly concerned with ourselves prevents us from making sacrifices and giving to our wives. But what does a lack of sacrifice and giving look like? Here are two situations that illustrate a lack of sacrifice and giving.

Two Common Failures in Sacrificial Love

First, **prioritizing your values over those of your wife** can hinder your ability to make sacrifices for her. For instance, I once saw a movie with a scene where the husband responded to a frightening encounter with a burglar in quite an embarrassing and disgraceful manner. The husband and his wife were asleep at 2 am when the wife heard a noise coming from downstairs that woke her up. She nudged her husband to wake him up and frantically said, "Wake up! I believe someone is in our house!" So they hurriedly got out of bed, and the husband slowly tiptoed down the stairs with a small flashlight in his hands, with his wife standing close behind him. Once they reached the bottom of the stairs, they saw no signs of an intruder. They experienced a moment of relief. Then, suddenly, a masked man appeared, holding a gun at them, demanding money and threatening to shoot them. The husband pleads with the man not to shoot. As the burglar moved towards them, the husband, being overcome by fear, snatched his wife from behind him and placed her in front of himself to use her as a human shield.

The husband told the burglar where the money was located. The burglar quickly took the cash and left their home, leaving the husband and wife unharmed. For my wife and me, this screen was a jaw-dropper. We both looked in awe and in disbelief at what we were seeing. What are your thoughts about this story? If you were facing a burglar in your home and you responded the same way as the husband in the movie, how would your wife feel or react if you did that to her? What was wrong with how the husband responded? What compelled him to use his wife as a human shield? He was more concerned about his own life than he was about his wife. He violated Ephesians 5:25. Instead of sacrificing his life for his wife, he was willing to sacrifice his wife for his life. He failed to love his wife because he loved himself more than her. On the contrary to loving oneself, Scripture says, "Greater love has no one than this, that one lay down his life for his friends." (Jn 15:13).

Of course, you may not ever attempt to use your wife as a human shield. That may be extreme. But is there anything you value in life more than your wife? For instance, I enjoy watching Monday Night Football. Moreover, some of my favorite activities include fishing out on the boat, playing golf with my golfing buddy on Saturdays, walking in the park, playing chess online with players worldwide, and spending time on my computer writing or doing ministry activities. I value these activities because I enjoy them; some are therapeutic and rewarding after a long work week. But there are times when I make these things a priority. I found myself spending more time enjoying what I loved rather than enjoying time with my wife. I must confess that there have been times when I sacrificed my wife for things I value.

What about you? Do you enjoy certain hobbies or activities so much that you attempt to enjoy them at your wife's expense? Embracing what you value as more important than your wife is rooted in an unwillingness to make sacrifices for her. And when there are moments that you give up your pleasures to make a sacrifice, you may be tempted to do it grudgingly. The lack of sacrifice also equates to the lack of giving. An unwillingness to give is an unwillingness to love.

Second, giving excessively to others—even in the name of doing good—can prevent you from giving adequately to your own spouse. Consider the case of a well-known multisite megachurch pastor who served faithfully for 37 years. Under his leadership, the church experienced exponential growth and became a vibrant presence in the community, known for its commitment to biblical counseling and support for those in need. He was deeply involved in the biblical counseling movement and served on the boards of several ministry organizations. Despite these outward successes, the pastor was ultimately asked to resign by the associate pastors and deacons due to allegations of being unloving toward his wife. This decision followed an email from his wife to church leaders, revealing that she and their children had moved out because of his emotional neglect. The church leadership concluded that he was no longer qualified for pastoral leadership.

Although he was respected as a counselor, visionary, and minister, he failed in his most personal calling—as a husband. How did this happen? He prioritized ministry over marriage. While there's no indication that he was unfaithful to his wife, his ministry became his mistress. Though his work was admirable, it consumed the time, energy, and affection that should have also been invested in his marriage. Warning signs were likely present, but he ignored them. Ultimately, he did not love his wife as Christ loved the church—through sacrifice and self-giving. It's possible he poured so much of himself into the lives of others that he had nothing left for his own family.

A few husbands spend a lot of time performing activities that are either enjoyable or productive. Some husbands are heavily involved in ministry or hold ministerial or pastoral positions in their Churches. Serving in the ministry is praiseworthy. Others are committed to helping their extended family members who are struggling. They are the "go-to" person whenever someone needs help. Most Go-to men see themselves as rescuers. Then there are those good Samaritan husbands who are passionate about spending their time in community service, helping neighbors, friends, and even strangers. They may also have a passion for getting involved in service projects. But most husbands are committed to their jobs and work hard to provide for their families. Husbands may become so involved in good activities, ministry, and their occupation that they neglect their wives. Like the pastor in the previous story, their marriage is damaged because they gave so much of themselves, their time, and energy to their jobs or engaging in good deeds for others that they neglected to give themselves to their wife.

Remedies for a Lack of Sacrificial Giving

What is the remedy for the lack of sacrifice and giving?

Pay Attention to Warning Signs

One remedy for the lack of sacrifice and giving is to pay attention to the warning signs. Most vehicles have an LED alert called a "check engine light" built into the dashboard, which is visible to the driver. There are sensors throughout the car that are designed to send messages to the check engine light if something malfunctions. The purpose of the "check engine light" is to illuminate and warn the driver of a potential problem with the engine that needs attention. A driver who ignores these warning signs and continues driving the vehicle may pay the price for it when it eventually breaks down.

If you are going to love your wife as Christ loved the church, you must be aware of the "check engine lights" in the marriage. You must live with your wife in an understanding way, but you cannot do this if you ignore the warning signs. But what are the warning signs of a problem in your marriage that must be addressed? Here are just a few examples: feeling disconnected, complaints, bad attitudes, frustration, lack of intimacy, avoidance, and isolation. A warning sign occurs when your wife shows disapproval through her facial expressions when you are sharing your planned activities that don't involve her. Another warning sign could be that she frequently questions your whereabouts. Or your attempt to have general conversations with her that turn into arguments. Other signs could include children or teenagers who are out of control because of a lack of discipline. Finally, neglected home maintenance could also be a sign of a problem.

If you are still trying to figure out warning signs in your marriage, here is an easy fix. Consider the following question for a moment: What does your wife complain about the most? A common pet peeve among some husbands is that their wives complain too much. Some also grumble about the tone in which the wives present their complaints. Many of these men view their wives' approach to presenting their complaints as disrespectful. So, I challenged these husbands by asking them, "The tone of your wife's voice may have been inappropriate and disrespectful. Let's forget about how she presented the complaint. The question is, is what your wife is saying to you true?" In many cases, the husband will answer this question with, "Yes." The point is that your wife may not always present her concerns in a loving manner. Her tone of voice may be inappropriate. Her facial expressions may not be the most beautiful. But whenever she has a complaint, I want to encourage you always to take time to ponder what she has said and ask yourself, "Is what my wife is saying true? And if what she is saying is true, then what am I, as her loving servant leader, going to do to fix it, to make it right?" But what is it that may keep us from responding to our wives' complaints in this manner? Pride. Sometimes, a husband can focus so much on receiving respect and affirmation from his wife that he experiences missed opportunities to sacrifice, give, or serve her due to a lack of humility. He wants his wife to serve him rather than him rendering service to her.

Another common tendency among some husbands is to respond to their wives' complaints with silence. Rather than engaging in dialogue, they choose to listen quietly and say nothing, hoping to keep the peace. However, this silence is not always a sign of resolution. While the husband may appear calm on the outside, he may often internalize his frustration, which can gradually turn into resentment or contempt toward his wife. Eventually, a seemingly minor comment or action from her may trigger an explosive reaction from her husband. Confused by the intensity of her husband's outburst, the wife wonders why his response is so disproportionate. This kind of internalized bitterness is especially harmful in a marriage. When left unaddressed, it can severely damage the relationship once it inevitably surfaces. That's why the apostle Paul exhorts, "Husbands, love your wives and do not be embittered against them" (Colossians 3:19).

Just as you take off and put on your shoes, if you are going to love your wife by sacrificing through giving, you must put to death bitterness and put on love. You must intentionally put to death pride and put on humility. In other words, you must exhibit the character of Christ. Although Jesus was God in the flesh, he humbled himself to a mere man. In Philippians 2:5-7, the apostle Paul challenges us to,

"Have this attitude in yourselves which was also in Christ Jesus, who, although He existed in the form of God, did not regard equality with God a thing to be grasped, but emptied Himself, taking the form of a bond-servant, and being made in the likeness of men."

Like Christ, if you are going to love your wife by sacrifice and giving, then you must empty yourself and walk in humility by serving her. Get rid of all pride and bitterness by confessing your sins to God and asking for forgiveness. Pay attention to the warning signs and respond lovingly. But if you are going to respond biblically to the warning signs, it may require reprioritizing your life.

Reprioritize Your Life

Prioritizing your life is the second remedy for the lack of sacrifice and giving. You may need to establish priorities if you want to love your wife as Christ loved the Church through sacrifice and giving. The following is a list of practical steps to reprioritize your life.

1. Make a list of all of your activities during a typical week.

2. Identify and distinguish between wants, desires, and needs.

3. Separate and place each activity into one of the following two categories:

- Activities that are pleasurable but not a priority.

- Activities are beneficial to you and your wife.

4. In what ways are each of those activities in question #3 beneficial to you and your wife?

5. Can some activities that are not necessarily beneficial to your wife be postponed until another time?

6. What reasonable sacrifice will you make to spend more time with your wife?

7. Survey your home and identify home improvements or repairs around the house that need attention (e.g., cleaning out or reorganizing the garage, trimming trees and shrubs, pressure washing the driveway, cleaning out the gutters, repairing leaky faucets/toilets, replacing light bulbs/fixtures, etc.).

- Ask your wife to list what's needed around the house that you may have missed.

- Schedule specific dates on the kitchen calendar (or somewhere visible to you and your wife) when you plan to complete each task.

Note 1: Intentionally scheduling time to get things done around the house is practical and commendable. Your wife will love you for it. But here is a caveat: Saying, "I'll get to it when I can," is insufficient. Setting dates to complete tasks is a means of accountability. However, the repair/home improvement schedule should not be "ironclad." The schedule is simply a tentative plan. So, if, for some reason, you cannot complete the task according to the specified date, let your wife know and reschedule it.

Be intentional in scheduling quality time with your children (e.g., sharing the gospel with them, instructing them in the Word of God, Helping with school homework, going to sports events, taking a walk with them individually, asking questions concerning their friends, goals, college plans, fears, worries, and struggles, and sharing your own similar life experiences that you had when you were their age). Take time to remind your children how much you love them. If you love them, then tell them so.

Be Intentional in Making Sacrifices

Lastly, scheduling time, making sacrifices, and giving to your wife will transform your marriage. You can schedule date nights and write them on a calendar. Spend quality time with your wife and be intentional. Let her know that you are willing to cancel some of your planned activities to spend time doing what she enjoys.

As discussed in the previous chapter, loving your wife as Christ loved the church means living with her in wisdom and understanding. A practical way to do this is to ask what she enjoys. Here are a few romantic activities your wife might appreciate: going to the movies or her favorite restaurants, enjoying candlelight dinners at home, window shopping at the mall, attending a theatrical play (such as The Lion King) or a concert, taking a dinner cruise, planning an annual vacation, or escaping for a weekend getaway at a bed and breakfast in another city. She might also enjoy spending time at the beach, having a picnic there, or even getting a foot spa together at a nail salon. Taking walks in the park is another simple but meaningful way to connect. The key is to be intentional. Make an effort to schedule quality time with your wife. Sacrificing your time and energy to invest in your relationship is one of the most tangible ways to show her love.

Conclusion

Loving your wife as Christ loved the church requires sacrifice through giving. Sure, confessing that we have all said or done things we wish we could take back is essential. We all have regrets because of misplaced priorities. But there is always hope, no matter the struggles in your marriage or how often you or your wife have been hurt by what the other person has said or done. Your marriage is never beyond repair. Restoration and reconciliation are available, but it starts with you. Loving your wife as Christ loved the church by sacrifice through giving creates an opportunity to live at peace with God and with your wife.

Ephesians 5:2-3, "Therefore be imitators of God, as beloved children; and walk in love, just as Christ also loved you and gave Himself up for us, an offering and a sacrifice to God as a fragrant aroma."

My challenge is that you make every effort to imitate Christ and cultivate a lifestyle of loving your wife by giving yourself up as an offering and sacrifice to the Lord. When you do, you will find favor with God as a sweet aroma in his nostrils. Sure, God knows that we are not perfect. God does not expect us to be perfect. But he does expect us to be growing.

If you have fallen short of loving your wife by sacrifice and giving, pray the following:

Pray: Lord, I confess to you and my wife that I have failed to love her as Christ loved the church through sacrifice and giving. Please forgive me for my sins and for failing to do what you commanded me to do as a husband. Lord, you have done so much for me that I do not deserve. Therefore, Lord, help me imitate your Son, Jesus Christ, as one of your chosen children. And help me, by the power of your Holy Spirit, to walk in love, just as Christ also loved me and gave himself up for me, an offering and sacrifice to you, Lord, as a fragrant aroma. So please help me give up myself as an offering and sacrifice to you and my wife as a fragrant aroma. In Jesus' name, Amen.

Reflection Questions

1. What is one area of your life where selfishness often prevents you from sacrificing for your wife?

2. What "warning signs" in your marriage have you ignored that may point to a lack of giving and sacrifice?

3. How can you practically reprioritize your schedule this week to demonstrate sacrificial love toward your wife?

4. When was the last time your wife was genuinely surprised or moved by a sacrifice you made for her? What could you do to create another moment like that soon?

Chapter 3
Loving Your Wife as Christ Loved the Church Requires Humility

"Do You Know Who I Am?"

There is a story about a Drug Enforcement Administration (DEA) officer who stopped at a ranch in Texas to talk with an old rancher about the need to inspect his property.

The DEA officer told the rancher, *"I need to inspect your ranch for illegally grown drugs."*

Holding his hand up and pointing his finger in a specific direction, the rancher said, *"Okay, but don't go in that field over there."*

The DEA officer verbally exploded, saying, *"Mister, I have the authority of the Federal Government with me!"*

Reaching into his rear pants pocket, he removed his badge, proudly displayed it to the rancher, and said, *"See this badge? This badge means I can go wherever I wish, on any land!! No questions asked or answers given!! Have I made myself clear? Do you understand?"*

The rancher nodded politely, apologized, and went about his chores.

A short time later, the old rancher suddenly heard screams, looked up, and saw the DEA officer running for his life, being chased by the rancher's big Santa Gertrudis bull.

With every step, the bull was gaining ground on the officer, and it seemed likely that he'd be gored before he reached safety. The officer was terrified.

Seeing that the DEA was in serious trouble, the rancher threw down his tools, ran to the fence, and yelled at the top of his lungs, *"QUICK...YOUR BADGE, SHOW HIM YOUR BADGE!!"*

This story is hilarious. But here are a few key points of the story worth noting. Initially, the DEA officer was prideful and arrogant about his position of authority. The officer asserted authority over the farmer because of pride. His prideful attitude compelled him to attempt to judge the motives behind the farmer's advice, as he believed the farmer was trying to restrict his governmental authority. In pride, the officer rejected the wise counsel of the farmer even though the farmer's warning was in the officer's best interest. The point of the story is that no matter how much authority a person believes he has, there will be times when one's perceived authority is worthless in the presence of someone with greater authority. The story's irony lies in the fact that the farmer had authority over the bull, the DEA officer had authority over the farmer, and the bull proclaimed authority over the DEA officer. If only the DEA officer had humbled himself and taken the farmer's advice, he would not have gotten into trouble.

What does the story of the DEA officer, the farmer, and the raging bull have to do with husbands? Some of us may hold up our manhood and position of husband as a badge of entitlement and authority. However, if we are not careful, we can easily allow our pride to compel us to assert authority over our wives in ways that God never intended. Pride is the most dangerous of all sins because it is the most blinding of all sins, and those who struggle with pride the most cannot see it, even when others bring it to their attention. Someone once said that "pride is to compete for supremacy with God with a heart (attitude) that has turned against the things of God." In other words, pride says, "I believe in God, but I have freedom of choice. I know what God's Word says, but my way is better. Besides, doing everything that God asks is just too difficult." This mindset depicts the epitome of pride. But pride is not just an attitude.

Pride is also an action that may show up, especially in how we relate to our wives. Pride can cause us to attempt to judge our wives' motives. Pride can also lead us to reject the wise counsel of our wives, even when what they are saying to us is in our best interest. Pride (the lack of humility) can prevent us from listening to our wife's advice, opinions, and suggestions concerning what we should or should not do (like the wise advice that the farmer offered to the officer). Then, we find ourselves in trouble, which results from our poor decisions. For these reasons, it is essential to put to death all manifestations of pride in our hearts and pursue humility as we seek to love our wives as Christ loved the church.

While it is true that husbands are God-ordained authorities in the home, we are still under God's authority, and he will hold us accountable. As such, husbands must exercise their authority not with pride and arrogance but in a spirit of humility. Since humility is one of Christ's attributes, we are commanded to reflect Christ's humility. We must relate to our wives with gentleness and humility.

This chapter shows that loving your wife as Christ loved the church requires humility. Our most remarkable example of humility is seen in the life of Christ.

Christ, Our Model of Humility

Philippians 2:5-8 provides the ultimate example of humility,

"Have this attitude in yourselves which was also in Christ Jesus, who, although He existed in the form of God, did not regard equality with God a thing to be grasped, but emptied Himself, taking the form of a bond-servant, and being made in the likeness of men. Being found in appearance as a man, He humbled Himself by becoming obedient to the point of death, even death on a cross."

According to Philippians 2:5-8, Christ was fully aware of his divine nature and position before God. Yet he chose to leave his heavenly position and lowered (emptied) himself to a mere man through humility and obedience to the Father, even until death. Christ's attitude is the epitome of humility and obedience. But how is "humility" defined, and what does it look like, practically, regarding how a husband should relate to his wife?

What is Humility?

Humility is the state of lowliness, especially in one's view of self in relation to others. Writer Stuart Scott defined humility as "The mindset of Christ (a servant's mindset); a focus on God and others, a pursuit of the recognition and exaltation of God, and a desire to glorify and please God in all things and by all things He has given."[1] In other words, Scott says that humility occurs when one focuses on God and others to glorify and exalt the Lord. Jerry Bridges said, "When a believer is truly humble before God and His word, he will also be humble about his own gifts, abilities, and attainments. He will realize and gratefully acknowledge that all that he is and all that he has comes from the hand of God."[2]

Furthermore, the word "Humble" appears 89 times in Scripture, 69 times in the Old Testament, and 20 times in the New Testament. The various meanings of humble in the Old Testament include to bend, crouch down, lay low, submit, or be brought down by affliction to a lowly position. In the New Testament, humility is "a condition of low estate which will be brought about through the judgment of God....or spirit of lowliness which enables God to bring the blessing of advancement."[3]

In Matthew 23:12, Jesus emphasized the significance of humility by saying, "Whoever exalts himself shall be humbled, and whoever humbles himself shall be exalted." In Matthew 23:12, Jesus was speaking publicly about the idea of what defines "greatness." Although Jesus spoke this profound statement directly to the crowd, he was also addressing the Pharisees, whom he knew were within hearing distance. What was the problem with the Pharisees that Jesus was addressing? The Pharisees lacked humility. They were prideful, self-righteous, and misunderstood the true meaning of greatness. The Pharisees believed that being served by others and receiving praise and recognition from men was evidence of one's greatness. They dressed well to be seen by men because, to them, their outer appearance was of great value and an avenue for receiving compliments (Matt. 23:5). The Pharisees sounded trumpets when giving to people experiencing poverty to be noticed by men (Matt. 6:2). They prayed aloud on the corners of busy streets so that others could see them coming and going (Matt. 6:5). The Pharisees were more concerned about men's approval than God's approval. They wanted to be esteemed by men rather than God. Jesus warned his disciples, the Pharisees, and all believers today that whoever exalts or elevates himself will be made low through disappointment (Matt. 23:12). In other words, the one who lifts himself in pride will be brought down.

On the other hand, Jesus says that the opposite is true of those who are humble. Jesus says, "Whoever humbles himself shall be exalted." In essence, Jesus says that the person who consistently humbles himself will be consistently exalted by God and sometimes others. For instance, my close cousin, Steve, is always doing good and serving others. He is a large company executive with an annual income of over six figures. Yet Steve has a reputation for being humble, loving, and having a gentle spirit. He has portrayed these character traits since we were children. Steve easily weeps with those who weep and rejoices with those who rejoice. Steve loves and worships the Lord, ensuring his household does the same. He is the caregiver for his elderly parents and other family members who require assistance. Humility is part of who Steve is. He demonstrates humility in his attitude and his actions by giving and serving others. Steve's character reflects Christ's humility. His life displayed the English Puritan Thomas Watson's definition of humility when he said, "A humble soul is emptied of all swelling thoughts of himself." [4]

My fellow husbands, are you emptied of all swelling thoughts of yourself? This question is convicting even as I write these words. But we are all a work in progress. Moving forward, now that you know the definitions of humility, how does it look in practice? What can you do to regularly and continuously love your wife as Christ loved the church by exhibiting a spirit of humility?

Humility in Practice

Bridges wrote, "Humility in every area of life, in every relationship with other people, begins with a right concept of God as the One who is infinite and eternal in His majesty and holiness." [5] In other words, humility in every area of your life and your relationship with your wife begins with having a proper view of God. Like wisdom and understanding that we discussed in chapter 1, humility is a by-product of knowing and embracing God. Having a proper view of God gives you a proper view of self.

Moreover, if you are going to exhibit humility, there are a few things you need to stop doing (we will call these things "Put-offs") and things that you need to start doing (we will call these " put-ons"). Real change does not occur simply by discontinuing a specific behavior. A desired change happens when you replace bad habits with good ones. Do you want to cultivate a spirit of humility in how you relate to your wife? Do you want to be exalted by the Lord? Here are some practical applications that will facilitate your spiritual growth in humility.

Practical Steps for Walking in Humility

Step 1: Identify the attributes of pride that influence your relationship with your wife and replace them with humility in both attitude and actions. Below is a list of examples of pride that you may need to put off, along with corresponding characteristics of humility that you need to put on. Review the list of put-offs and put-ons below. Read the description of each and the corresponding scriptures. Identify which attributes of pride and humility are applicable/relevant to you. Which ones do you struggle with? Are there areas where you need improvement? Are there some attributes that you need to grow in and exhibit more often? Once you have identified which attributes of humility you need to improve, write the corresponding Scripture on an index card and keep it where you can see it regularly.

Step 2: Create four columns on an 8 x 11 sheet of paper. In the first column, write the selected Scripture verbatim. In the second column, list keywords from the selected text, look up each word in a dictionary, and briefly define each keyword. Then, summarize what the passage means in one sentence. Write the meaning of the passage at the top of the third column. List at least seven to ten specific ways you can apply this passage to your life, specifically how you relate to your wife. In other words, list seven to ten things you can do to change. Finally, in the fourth column, write out a personalized prayer that includes the passage in the prayer, asking God to help you put this passage into practice. Commit the Scripture to memory and quote it at least three times a day for seven consecutive days. The following is a list of "Put-offs" and "Put-ons."

A. Put off being self-focused and put on being Christ-focused.

> Colossians 3:1-3, "Therefore, if you have been raised with Christ, keep seeking the things that are above, where Christ is, seated at the right hand of God. Set your minds on the things that are above, not on the things that are on earth. For you have died, and your life is hidden with Christ in God."

A humble husband is Christ-centered rather than self-centered. He seeks to glorify God by conforming to the image of his Son, Jesus Christ. He takes the time to examine his heart to ensure that his thoughts, attitudes, and actions are pleasing to the Lord.

B. Put off esteeming yourself above your wife and put on esteeming your wife as better than yourself.

> Phil. 2:3-4, "Do nothing from selfishness or empty conceit, but with humility consider one another as more important than yourselves; do not merely look out for your own personal interests, but also for the interests of others."

A humble husband values his wife more than himself because he can see his own heart better than he can see hers.[6]

C. Put off responding with anger to your wife's constructive criticism and put on acceptance of her reproof and reproach.

> Proverbs 9:8, "Do not rebuke a scoffer, or he will hate you; Rebuke a wise person, and he will love you."

Reproof and reproach are synonyms, but are slightly different. Reproof is a stern, direct rebuke, harsher criticism often to correct bad behavior, and reproach is a milder, gentler expression of disapproval. Thomas Watson wrote, "Reproof to a proud man is like pouring water on lime, which grows hotter. A gracious soul loves the one who reproves. The humble-spirited Christian can bear the reproach of an enemy and the reproof of a friend.[7]

D. Put off self-righteousness and put on appreciation for God's grace.

> Ephesians 2:8-9, "For by grace you have been saved through faith, and this is not of yourselves, it is the gift of God; not a result of works, so that no one may boast."

A humble husband sees himself as the worst of sinners. He acknowledges his unrighteousness and his unworthiness of God's grace. Because of his self-awareness and gratitude for God's grace, he is willing to extend grace to his wife, especially when injured or offended.

E. Put off impatience and put on gentleness and patience.

> Ephesians 4:1-2, "Therefore I, the prisoner of the Lord, urge you to walk in a manner worthy of the calling with which you have been called, with all humility and gentleness, with patience, bearing with one another in love,"

A humble husband is long-suffering and tolerates his wife's imperfections and frailties. He maintains self-restraint under provocation and addresses his wife's wrongs with tenderness and compassionate correction.

F. Put off being a poor listener and put on being an attentive listener.

> James 1:19, "You know this, my beloved brothers and sisters. Now, everyone must be quick to hear, slow to speak, and slow to anger."

A humble husband is more concerned about understanding his wife than being understood. He listens attentively when his wife is speaking to gain an understanding of what she is trying to communicate. A humble husband not only listens to what his wife says, but he also listens to her with his heart. He recognizes that his responsibility as a husband is to "live with his wife in an understanding way" (1 Peter 3:7). So he is not only seeking to understand what she is saying, but he seeks to understand what she is feeling.

G. Put off thinking that your way is the only way and put on valuing your wife's opinion.

> Proverbs 18:1-2, "An unfriendly person pursues selfish ends and against all sound judgment starts quarrels. Fools find no pleasure in understanding but delight in airing their own opinions" (NIV).

A humble husband acknowledges that he does not know it all. He values his wife's opinions even though her thinking pattern may not fit his logic. A humble husband values his wife's input and does not denounce her opinion. He sometimes agrees to try doing things according to his wife's suggestions. Embracing your wife's ideas does not mean you relinquish your authority as the head of your home. I am also not suggesting that you always wait until your wife agrees before moving forward with a decision you believe is in the family's best interest. As the leader of the home, you will occasionally have to make decisions that your wife may not always agree with. But a humble husband recognizes that his wife's ideas are of great worth, even when her ideas do not align with his. If he agrees with his wife and later discovers her advice is wrong, the humble husband does not rub it in her face.

H. Put off communicating words that tear down your wife and put on communicating words that build her up.

> Ephesians 4:29, " Let no unwholesome word proceed from your mouth, but only such a word as is good for edification according to the need of the moment, so that it will give grace to those who hear."

A humble husband avoids using words that could tear his wife down, instead using words that edify and graciously build her up.

I. Put off the demand to be served and put on being committed to serving your wife.

> Mark 10:45, "For even the Son of Man did not come to be served, but to serve, and to give His life a ransom for many."

A humble husband is more concerned about serving his wife than being served. He is akin to an exceptional server in a fine-dining restaurant who always asks, "How may I serve you? What would you like? Is there anything else I can do for you?"

J. Put off being defensive and put on admitting your faults.

> James 5:16, "Therefore, confess your sins to one another, and pray for one another so that you may be healed. The effective prayer of a righteous man can accomplish much."

Sometimes, being defensive when approached about a fault is a vehicle that some people use to manipulate the conversation by flipping the issue back to the accuser. Defensiveness is used to deflect and avoid being exposed or admitting to wrong or accusation by pointing the finger back at the presenter of the problem. Many of us may be tempted to become defensive because the tone with which our wives present the problem is not always the greatest. A wise husband should later address his concern about tone with his wife with compassionate correction. But a humble husband avoids being defensive, admits his faults, and takes responsibility for his actions. He prays for himself and his wife. Scott wrote that a humble person responds to admonishment with, "I was wrong. You were right. Thank you for telling me."[8]

K. Put off withholding forgiveness and be willing to grant and ask for forgiveness.

> Colossians 3:13, "bearing with one another, and forgiving each other, whoever has a complaint against anyone; just as the Lord forgave you, so also should you."

A humble person is willing to forgive others because he recognizes the magnitude of Christ's forgiveness towards him. A humble husband does not harbor bitterness and resentment towards his wife for the wrongs she committed against him (Col. 3:19). He readily grants to his wife and asks for forgiveness from his wife because he realizes how much he has been forgiven in Christ. He realizes that he and his wife are both sinners who said, "I DO." As such, a humble husband quickly extends mercy to his wife, even if it is not reciprocated. And, of course, forgiveness takes more time for some than others. Nevertheless, we should not prolong forgiveness.

L. Rather than trying to cover up your shortcomings, be open and honest about the areas where you need to grow.

> Matthew 7:3-4, "Why do you look at the speck that is in your brother's eye, but do not notice the log that is in your own eye? Or how can you say to your brother, 'Let me take the speck out of your eye,' and behold, the log is in your own eye?"

We can easily identify imperfections, faults, and sins in our wives' attitudes, words, and actions. But it is easy to overlook our own flaws, faults, and sins. It is even easier for us to maximize our wives' wrongs and shortcomings while minimizing our own. Proverbs 16:2 explains why this is our tendency when it says, "All the ways of a man are clean in his own sight, but the Lord weighs the motives."

The natural, sinful inclinations of our hearts compel us to see ourselves as better than we truly are. But a humble person is mindful of his own heart's sinful, self-righteous inclinations. A humble husband views his wife's sin as equal to his own sin against God and others. He views sin as sin. A humble husband does not view his wife's sin as greater or less than his own. When he does address his wife's sin, he does so by confessing to her and addressing his own.

Completing this application assignment will help you cultivate a spirit of humility as you seek to love your wife as Christ loved the church.

Conclusion

Loving your wife as Christ loved the church requires humility. Do not be like the DEA officer in the story, who is prideful and arrogant about his position of authority and judges the motives of others. Avoid being a husband who rejects your wife's wise counsel even though you know she has your best interest at heart. Instead, reflect Christ's humility: listen, serve, forgive, and esteem your wife above yourself. Remember that it is essential to put all manifestations of pride residing in your heart to death and pursue humility as you seek to love your wife as Christ loved the church. Since humility is one of Christ's attributes, you are commanded to reflect Christ's humility. You must relate to your wife with wisdom, understanding, and humility. Humility is not about thinking less of yourself — it's about thinking of yourself less, so that you can love your wife more.

As we'll see in the next chapter, humility naturally leads to gentleness and mercy — more essential Christlike qualities that you need to love your wife.

Reflection Questions

1. In what ways has pride shown up in how you relate to your wife — through defensiveness, dismissing her counsel, or insisting on your way?

2. Which "put off / put on" practice from this chapter do you most need to focus on right now in your marriage?

3. How can you begin listening to your wife not only with your ears but with your heart this week?

4. What is one practical act of humility you can show your wife in the next seven days?

Chapter 4

Loving Your Wife as Christ Loved the Church Requires Gentleness and Mercy

Gentleness and mercy are character qualities that you must exhibit if you are going to love your wife as Christ loved the church. Loving your wife requires gentleness and mercy.

Gentleness in Scripture

First, loving your wife as Christ loved the church requires gentleness. What is gentleness according to Scripture? In the Bible, gentleness means to express kindness towards another with tenderness. Gentleness also has several shades of meaning, including mildness, humility, meekness, courtesy, and forbearance.[1] Gentleness is an attribute of the character of Jesus. The prophet Isaiah wrote,

> "Like a shepherd He [Jesus] will tend His flock, In His arm He will gather the lambs And carry them in His bosom; He will gently lead the nursing ewes" (Isa. 40:11).

In setting the context of Isaiah 40:11, the prophet proclaims the Omnipotent God who will rescue and deliver his chosen people from captivity and lead them to glory. The writer refers to Jesus as the Shepherd and Ruler of His sheep. As the Shepherd-ruler of his sheep, Isaiah said that Jesus tends to them, gathers them, carries them, and leads them with gentleness. Isaiah speaks of Jesus' gentleness in dealing with God's chosen people, likening it to the tenderness of a Shepherd who cares for his sheep.

A husband who seeks to love his wife as Christ loved the church must lead her with gentleness and express kindness toward her with the tenderness of a Shepherd who cares for his sheep.

The Gospels also speak of the gentleness of Jesus. In the gospel of Matthew, Jesus said,

> "Take My yoke upon you and learn from Me, for I am gentle and humble in heart, and you will find rest for your souls. [30]"For My yoke is easy and My burden is light." (Matt. 11:29-30).

In Matthew 11:29-30, Jesus says that gentleness and humility are not merely outward expressions of his behavior but rather deep-seated emotions of his heart. He exhibits gentleness and humility, which are attributes of his divine nature. But meekness and gentleness, in our culture, are grossly minimized and misunderstood.

Meekness: Misunderstood Strength

Interestingly, "gentleness" is also closely akin to "meekness." There is a contrast between our culture and the biblical definition of "meekness." First, the term "meekness" carries a slightly negative connotation in our culture. According to the Merriam-Webster Dictionary, meek is defined as "deficient in spirit and courage, submissive." Merriam-Webster describes the characteristic of a meek person as one who lacks spirit and courage.

Furthermore, the British dictionary defines meekness as a lack of spine or a tendency to be compliant or unassertive. Other dictionaries define "meekness" as soft, weak, or lacking self-assurance. Our culture mainly views meekness as a weakness rather than a strength. Today, many social media platforms, popular movies, and entertainment sitcoms portray heroes as exercising power and strength to avenge, defeat, and conquer their enemies. Meekness is viewed as cowardice.

On the other hand, Scripture describes "meek" or meekness" quite differently than our culture. The King James Version of the Bible employs the word "meek" or "meekness" instead of "gentle or gentleness" 31 times. While gentleness and meekness are closely related, there is a subtle difference.

Gentleness refers to a kind, tenderhearted interaction with others, and meekness refers to a humble, submissive attitude accompanied by self-restraint amid unjust suffering without retaliation. Meekness is characterized by an attitude that prioritizes the needs of others above one's own. Gentleness is a kind response, and meekness is the attitude of love and compassionate correction. Biblically, gentleness and meekness are virtues that Christians are commanded to exemplify. They are listed as characteristics of the Fruit of the Spirit (Gal. 5:23-24). Moreover, Jesus preached about the blessings of those who are gentle when he said, "Blessed are the gentle, for they shall inherit the earth" (Matt. 5:5). Jesus' life demonstrated the epitome of gentleness and meekness, especially when he experienced unjust treatment by his enemies. First Peter 2:22-23 says,

"He who committed no sin, nor was any deceit found in His mouth; and while being abusively insulted, He did not insult in return; while suffering, He did not threaten, but kept entrusting Himself to Him who judges righteously;"

How do gentleness and meekness apply to fulfilling your role as a husband and loving your wife? Gentleness and meekness are essential to loving your wife, as Christ loved the church. The test of gentleness and meekness occurs when you have been wronged or sinned against by your wife. What should you do when your wife sins against you? What do gentleness and meekness look like under these conditions? The apostle Paul wrote:

> "Brethren, even if anyone is caught in any trespass, you who are spiritual, restore such a one in a spirit of gentleness; each one looking to yourself, so that you too will not be tempted. [2] Bear one another's burdens, and thereby fulfill the law of Christ. [3] For if anyone thinks he is something when he is nothing, he deceives himself. [5] For each one will bear his own load (Gal. 6:1-3, 5).

Paul says, if a person (including your wife) has committed a sin or been caught in wrongdoing, you who are spiritually mature, wise, and understanding, restore the person with gentleness and humility while being mindful of your own shortcomings and propensity to commit the same trespasses.

Here is a true story that portrays a husband's gentle and meek response to being disrespected by his wife (their names have been changed to protect their identity).

Ben and Liz

Over two decades ago, when I was a deacon in training, my wife Cynthia and I were assigned to serve alongside an experienced deacon named Ben and his wife, Liz. They became our mentors for 2 ½ years, teaching us the rhythms of service, the humility of ministry, and the heart of leadership. From preparing the communion table to leading morning devotionals and visiting the sick and shut-in, we learned by walking with them. Over time, our relationship with Ben and Liz grew into a deep and lasting friendship.

I remember one moment during those early years that left a permanent impression on me. It was the first time my wife and I accompanied Ben and Liz to serve communion to members who were sick and unable to attend church. That morning, Ben drove, Liz sat in the front seat, and Cynthia and I were in the back. After visiting three members, we set out for our final stop.

On the freeway, Liz advised Ben, "You need to take the next exit." Ben quietly kept driving, choosing to pass the suggested exit and take the next one instead. Liz grew frustrated. With a raised tone, she said, "I can't believe you missed the exit. Now it's going to take us longer."

Ben calmly replied, "I think this way will be fine." But when he later made a U-turn and then turned onto a street Liz didn't recognize, her frustration boiled over. With an elevated voice, she snapped, "Now we're lost! Your problem is that you never listen. You're stubborn, and you think you know everything. Just do it your way—I don't care anymore."

The car went silent. Ben said nothing in response. Cynthia and I exchanged quiet glances in the back seat. Eventually, we reached our elderly church member's home, served communion, sang a praise song, prayed with our church member, and finished the visit. On the drive back, casual conversation slowly resumed as if nothing had happened.

But inside, I was wrestling. Why didn't Ben defend himself? Why would a man allow his wife to speak to him publicly that way without responding? At the time, shaped by cultural ideas about masculinity, I ascribed to Ben being a weak or passive husband.

I was wrong.

The very next Sunday, after church service, Ben and Liz pulled my wife and me aside. With tears in her eyes, Liz confessed her disrespect toward Ben and asked both him and us for forgiveness. She was sincerely repentant and ashamed of how she had acted. In that moment, I saw not weakness in Ben, but strength.

He had responded to conflict with restraint, gentleness, meekness, and love. He addressed the matter privately, not publicly, guiding his wife with compassion rather than retaliation.

That experience taught me a lesson about marriage and leadership that has stayed with me for more than thirty years. No marriage is perfect—every couple faces conflict. But Ben modeled what it means for a husband to love his wife as Christ loves the church (Ephesians 5:25): with patience, humility, and a meek spirit, even when wronged.

To this day, Cynthia and I remain close with Ben and Liz. We still share meals and fellowship. And whenever I think of that car ride experience, I no longer see a passive man. Ben displayed a man of strength, character, and Christlike love.

How do you employ gentleness and meekness in loving your wife? Ben's response is a good example of practicing the meekness of Jesus, as found in First Peter 2:23-24, and the compassionate, gentle correction of Galatians 6:1-3. Remember that gentleness is an expression of kindness, humility, and tenderness. You can display gentleness when your wife has offended you or when attempting to address her sin. You can respond to your wife with gentleness by using words of encouragement that build her up, especially in areas where she is weak and needs to grow.

As I stated earlier, meekness is akin to gentleness. Meekness is a submissive attitude characterized by self-restraint in the face of unjust suffering without resorting to retaliation. The submission associated with meekness does not refer to submitting to your wife but submission to God. It is an attitude of prioritizing your wife's needs above your own. How can you employ meekness when you are relating to your wife? You exhibit meekness by not responding in kind to her offenses. If her words are harsh or you feel insulted by something she has said, do not insult her in return. If she yells at you, do not yell back in return. If you respond with anger, harsh words, or insults, you and your wife are equally guilty of sinning against one another. Do not allow her sin to become your sin. Exercise meekness by maintaining an attitude of humility and self-restraint amid unjust suffering without retaliation.

I commend my friend Ben for being a living example of what it means to love his wife, as Christ loved the church by responding to her with gentleness and meekness. Liz's confession and pursuit of forgiveness were also praiseworthy. Ben's gentle and meek response to Liz led to a sincere confession, genuine repentance, giving, and granting forgiveness. Ben's loving response to Liz's offense restored their relationship.

Husbands, let's work on exhibiting gentleness and meekness when relating to our wives. Not only are gentleness and meekness essential to loving our wives, but they must also be accompanied by mercy.

Mercy is Essential to Loving Your Wife

Remember that loving your wife as Christ loved the church also requires mercy. What is mercy? How is mercy defined? A simple definition of mercy that the average person may embrace is that mercy is "not getting what you deserve." Moreover, Merriam-Webster defines mercy as 1). Compassion or forbearance, shown especially to an offender or one subject to one's power; 2). Imprisonment rather than death is imposed as a penalty for first-degree murder. Additionally, the Oxford Dictionary defines "mercy" as "Clemency and compassion shown to a person who is in a position of powerlessness or subjection, or to a person with no right or claim to receive kindness; kind and compassionate treatment in a case where severity is merited or expected, esp. in giving legal judgment or passing sentence." Although there are a variety of definitions of mercy in our English dictionaries, the English vocabulary does not provide a word that is diametrically equivalent to the Biblical meaning of "mercy."

The Biblical Definition of Mercy

In Scripture, mercy is much more meaningful and far more profound than our English definition. Mercy is more than withholding punishment from an offender. Biblical scholars Walter Ewell and Phillip Comfort said, "The biblical meaning of mercy is exceedingly rich and complex, as evidenced by the fact that several Hebrew and Greek words were used to express the concept." Consequently, numerous synonyms are employed in English translations of the Bible to convey the multifaceted dimensions of mercy, including "kindness," "loving-kindness," "goodness," "grace," "favor," "pity," "compassion," and "steadfast love." Prominent in mercy is the compassionate disposition to forgive offenders or adversaries and help or spare them in their sorry plight."[2] As you can see, the biblical word and meaning of mercy far exceed our English definition. One thing is sure: biblical mercy involves shades of open expressions of love. Therefore, here is a working definition of mercy:

"Mercy is a deep-seated love, compassion, and emotional concern for those who are underserved and in need, or for one who has a debt that they cannot pay. Moreover, mercy is rooted in compassion that motivates benevolent acts of kindness towards the sufferer who is unworthy to be helped."

The Dictionary of Biblical Imagery defines mercy best: "Mercy is aid rendered to someone miserable or needy, especially to someone who is either in debt or without claim to favorable treatment." Now, let's examine what mercy looks like in practice.

Mercy: Love in Action

Additionally, there are several occasions in the Bible where people in misery or distress cried out to Jesus as he passed by, saying, "Have mercy on me" (Matt. 15:22, 17:15, 20:31-32; Mk. 10:47). How did Jesus respond to people's pleas for mercy? Here are instances where Jesus showed mercy by rendering aid to someone miserable or needy, especially to someone in debt or without a claim to favorable treatment.

- Jesus showed mercy by raising Lazarus from the dead. Jesus wept, being aware that Lazarus, whom he loved, had died and seeing the grief of Lazarus's sister Mary. So, Jesus arrived at the tomb where they laid Lazarus's body, and he raised Lazarus from the dead (Jn. 11:1-44).

- Jesus displayed mercy by feeding the 5,000 with five fish and two loaves of bread (Jn. 6:11-14). Interestingly, the Bible does not state whether all of the recipients of fish and bread even thanked Jesus or left a tip for their meal.

- Jesus displayed mercy on ten lepers, but after being healed, only one returned to Jesus to thank and glorify him (Lk. 17:11-19).

- Jesus showed mercy by healing the man with the withered hand (Mk. 3:1-6).

- Jesus displayed mercy by preventing the woman who was caught in adultery from being stoned to death (Jn. 8:10-11).

- Jesus showed mercy by giving a blind man sight (Mk. 8:22-26).

- Jesus showed mercy to those crucifying him on the cross (Lk. 23:34)

- Jesus showed mercy by forgiving sin (Lk. 7:46-48).

- Jesus displayed mercy towards us by laying down his life for our sins (Rom. 5:6-11).

Were any of the individuals that Jesus showed mercy to miserable? How many of them were needy? Were any of them in debt? In other words, did any of them sin and were worthy of death? Any sin committed against God and others is to be indebted to God and others. Were any of them worthy of favorable treatment? All those to whom Jesus extended mercy were miserable or needy, in debt, and without claim to favorable treatment. Yet Jesus, driven by a heart of love and compassion, rendered aid to these individuals and received nothing from them in return.

Practical Steps to Show Mercy to Your Wife

Loving your wife as Christ loved the church requires mercy. If you are going to be merciful towards your wife, there are specific steps you must take. First, you need to examine yourself. Second, you must have a heart of love and compassion for your wife. Third, you must evaluate your wife to identify her specific needs. Fourth, you must render aid according to her needs. Fifth, encourage your wife and be her cheerleader. Lastly, since forgiveness is a prominent aspect of mercy, you must both ask for and grant forgiveness.

First, your ability to display mercy towards your wife must start with examining yourself. What are some of your needs, weaknesses, and shortcomings? Are there areas in your life where you need to grow in your spiritual walk with God? In what ways have you failed as a husband or father? Do you harbor unforgiveness and anger? How well do you communicate with your wife? Are there things that you have said or done that have hurt your wife? What specific sins have you committed against your wife? Are you miserable or needy, in debt, and without claim to favorable treatment? Are you a recipient of the mercy of Jesus? Absolutely. Here is the point. If Jesus has been merciful to you throughout your life, you must be merciful towards your wife. Recognizing your need for mercy is the first step to being merciful to your wife. Why? When you realize the magnitude of God's mercy towards you, it will produce a spirit of humility and compel you to have compassion for your wife in her failures and weaknesses. You realize that she is miserable or needy, in debt, without claim to favorable treatment, and in need of mercy, just like you.

Second, if you are going to display mercy towards your wife, you must have a heart of love and a compassionate response to her failures and sins. Compassion is an essential part of mercy. Jesus showed a heart of compassion for those in distress before responding with mercy and rendering aid. For instance, Matthew 9:36 says, "Seeing the crowds, He felt compassion for them, because they were distressed and downcast, like sheep without a shepherd."

In Matthew 9:36, the word compassion" is the Greek word *"splagchnizomai,"* meaning to be moved in one's bowels (deep on the inside). In other words, when Jesus gazed upon the crowd of afflicted, dejected people who were without hope, their condition broke his heart. Then Jesus asked his disciples to pray that God would send more workers to Shepherd, serve, and minister to people, like the crowd before him, who were miserable or needy, in debt, and without claim to favorable treatment, yet all of them needed mercy.

If you are going to exhibit mercy towards your wife, you must have a heart of compassion towards her, especially in your responses to her imperfections and sin. Avoid responding in anger, which is the natural inclination of the flesh. Usually, when a person responds with ungodly anger to the imperfections and wrongs of others, it is because he is prideful and self-centered. An unloving attitude, such as anger, compels one to become insensitive and merciless to the offender's needs, cultivating animosity.

But a heart of compassion towards your wife is rooted in your love for God, which produces humility that stems from realizing your own wretchedness and unworthiness of God's mercy and forgiveness. Like the apostle Paul said, "Here is a trustworthy saying that deserves full acceptance: Christ Jesus came into the world to save sinners—of whom I am the worst." 1 Tim. 1:15 (NIV). You and I are the worst of sinners. Yet Christ saved sinners like us and showed us mercy by dying on the cross. Let Paul's mindset be in you, and have compassion for your wife by being sensitive to her needs, imperfections, and failures. But do you know what your wife's needs are?

Third, you must evaluate your wife to identify her needs, weaknesses, and areas for improvement. Your evaluation of your wife should never be for condemnation but for edification. Here are a few simple questions to consider. Where can she grow in her spiritual walk with God? How can you help her become a better wife, mother, parent, and daughter? How can you help her in her relationships with others? Does she struggle with unforgiveness and anger? Are there any heart issues that need to be addressed? How well does she communicate with you? Are her words always respectful and gracious? You can learn your wife's needs by listening attentively to what she says. Jesus said, "The good person out of the good treasure of his heart brings forth what is good, and the evil person out of the evil treasure brings forth what is evil; for his mouth speaks from that which fills his heart." (Luke 6:45)

The words of our mouths reveal what is in our hearts. Are there any heart issues that need to be addressed, such as bitterness, anger, resentment, or unforgiveness? You can learn what your wife needs by listening to her words and paying attention to her nonverbal cues, such as her body language and facial expressions. When does her facial expression disapprove? When her facial or body language expresses disapproval, ask her to share her thoughts and feelings at that moment. Ignoring or minimizing the significance of your wife's halo data creates missed opportunities to learn about your wife, identify a need, and minister to her. In addition to observing your wife's words, facial expressions, and body language, please pay close attention to her behavior patterns in response to you in various situations. Are there times when she appears to avoid you? Are there times when she shuts down communicating with you? Does she avoid being intimate with you? During these occasions, ask her to share her heart with you. Let her know how much you love and value her. Remind her of your concern about your relationship and desire to make things right. Showing mercy requires examining yourself, having a heart of compassion, and evaluating your wife to identify her needs, weaknesses, and areas for growth. Knowledge is not enough. You must also render aid to address the issues you have identified.

Fourth, you must render aid according to her needs. After evaluating your wife and identifying her needs, weaknesses, and shortcomings, you must render aid by addressing these areas with compassionate corrections, which is essential to exhibiting mercy. Take the log out of your eye by admitting your faults and taking responsibility for your sins (Matt. 7:1-5). Speak the truth in love. Be a Godly example in each area. If you are asking your wife to forgive, then you must forgive. If you ask your wife to control her anger, then control your anger. If you ask your wife to avoid bad attitudes, you must do the same. If you want your wife to respect you, show her respect. If you want to receive affirmation from your wife, then give affirmation. If you want your wife to show you that she appreciates you, show her that you appreciate her. If you want your wife to give you grace when you make mistakes, then be gracious to her when she makes mistakes. As a leader in the home, you must set an example. It would be hypocritical of you to ask your wife to practice a Christian discipline that you are unwilling to practice yourself.

Fifth, become your wife's cheerleader. Be intentional about acknowledging any changes she has made, no matter how small, and any noticeable attempts to improve. If you ignore her progress, be critical, minimize her efforts, or make light of her attempts to make positive changes, she will likely give up trying. Above all, as you strive to love your wife as Christ loves the church by showing mercy and providing for her needs, ensure that you willingly and freely offer her grace when she fails, falls, or makes mistakes. Lastly, pray for your wife, yourself, and your marriage. Also, you can schedule time to pray with her. Scripture says, "Therefore, confess your sins to one another, and pray for one another so that you may be healed. The effective prayer of a righteous man can accomplish much." (James 5:16)

Be Christ-like, not only by extending mercy to your wife by rendering aid and praying for her, but also by granting forgiveness.

Lastly, since forgiveness is a prominent aspect of mercy, you must both ask for and grant forgiveness. But what does it mean to forgive? Some may believe that to forgive means to let go and release the guilty from punishment. Others say, "I can forgive but not forget." A few may say they will only forgive when they see the fruit or evidence of repentance. Still, others are feeling-oriented people who struggle with overcoming the hurt caused by the offender, so they find it difficult, if not impossible, to forgive. Since there are a variety of understandings among Christians of the meaning of forgiveness, let's take a moment to define what forgiveness is biblically. What is forgiveness according to Scripture? Elwell and Comfort said that forgiveness means "Pardon, involving the restoration of broken relationships, ceasing to feel resentment for wrongs and offenses."[3] Moreover, Ronald Youngblood says that forgiveness is "the act of excusing or pardoning others despite their slights, shortcomings, and errors."[4]

Forgiveness is primarily an act of God towards sinners, but it also applies to man in his relationship with his neighbor. In essence, forgiveness is to pardon a debt owed by another. As stated previously, to display mercy is to have a heart of compassion towards and to render aid to one who is needy, in debt, or has a debt that he cannot pay.

Six months after my wife Cynthia and I were married in 1985, we purchased our first home with a 30-year mortgage from First City Bank of Houston, now Chase Bank. Ten years later, with two children and a growing family, we bought a larger home and rented out the first one. The rental income covered the mortgage payments, and life went on as usual.

Fast forward to 2012. With just four years left on that first mortgage, I opened a letter from Chase that changed everything. As I stood in the kitchen reading it, I could hardly believe my eyes. I read it once. Twice. Three times. Finally, I handed it to Cynthia. After scanning it, she exclaimed, "You've got to be kidding me."

The letter stated:

> "We at Chase Bank are happy to inform you that the remainder of your mortgage is pardoned. The balance of approximately $7,800 is entirely forgiven. Please discontinue future payments. Enclosed is a refund check from your escrow account."

We were stunned. We had done nothing to earn this pardon. We didn't deserve it. Yet the debt was canceled—completely wiped away. It was a "Praise the Lord!" moment we'll never forget.

That experience with Chase is a vivid picture of forgiveness. When someone sins against another, they incur a debt. But the one who has been wronged has the power to release that debt—to forgive. Forgiveness is not about the offender deserving it; it's about choosing to pardon, just as Christ commands His followers (Luke 17:3–10).

- The apostle Paul wrote, "bearing with one another, and forgiving each other, whoever has a complaint against anyone; just as the Lord forgave you, so must you do also." (Col. 3:13)

Do you have any complaints against your wife? I am sure you do. We all do. Typically, a husband's complaints against his wife include things that he may also be reluctant to forgive. So, I encourage you to identify your specific complaints about your wife and, for each complaint, forgive her. But be mindful, though, that your wife may also have complaints about you. Even more than your wife's complaints about you, are there things you have done or said in your past that Jesus could complain about if he chose to do so? Most definitely. We all stand guilty before Jesus, yet he forgives us for all the wrongs we have done in the past, present, and future.

Being mindful of the magnitude of Christ's forgiveness towards you, you must grant her forgiveness for the past offenses and sins she committed against you that hurt or injured you. Ask and grant forgiveness. According to Ken Sande, forgiveness may be described as a decision to make four promises:[5]

1. I will not dwell on this incident.

2. I will not bring up this incident again and use it against you.

3. I will not talk to others about this incident.

4. I will not let this incident stand between us or hinder our personal *relationship.*

So to love your wife requires forgiveness.

Conclusion

Gentleness and mercy are essential for loving your wife as Christ loved the church. Gentleness shows itself in kind, tender responses. Meekness restrains retaliation. Mercy moves with compassion to meet needs, forgive, and restore.

Jesus promises to reward those who are merciful. He said, "Blessed are the merciful, for they shall receive mercy." (Matt. 5:7)

And He reminds us to be, "Be merciful, just as your Father is merciful." (Lk. 6:36)

When you extend gentleness and mercy to your wife, you reflect the love of Christ to her. It will strengthen your marriage and glorify God.

Now that we have discussed gentleness and mercy as essentials to loving your wife as Christ loved the church, we will discuss patience and longsuffering, which are also requirements for loving your wife, in the next chapter.

Reflection Questions

1. When was the last time you chose retaliation instead of gentleness with your wife? Did your response make the situation better or worse? How could you have responded differently?

2. In what specific areas does your wife most need mercy from you right now?

3. How can you practically "be her cheerleader" this week, affirming her growth instead of criticizing her shortcomings?

4. Is there a past offense you still hold against your wife? What step can you take today to forgive her fully?

Chapter 5

Loving Your Wife as Christ Loved the Church Requires Patience and Long-suffering

Do You Enjoy Waiting?

I have lived in Houston, Texas, for most of my life. But for the last 24 years, we have lived in Friendswood, only 20 miles from downtown Houston and 5 miles from the Houston City limits. Most people I talk to who live in Houston and are non-natives love it here. However, most non-Houstonians have one common complaint about Houston. The most common complaint is about the traffic. Traffic is a problem in Houston. One reason for the heavy traffic is that, over the last 2 decades, the population in suburban Cities surrounding

Houston has exploded. Many people commute from suburban Cities to work, and Downtown Houston serves as a gateway between home and work. Waiting in traffic is the norm for Houston drivers because most of them have learned to be patient. But for others, waiting in Houston traffic is an annoyance and a nightmare.

Waiting in traffic is one thing. But what about waiting for your wife? Waiting for her to finish getting ready, or even to get out of the car after arriving somewhere? Does it take her longer than you do to make a decision, and then, moments after making her decision, she changes her mind? Do her habits ever test your nerves? If I asked your wife whether you are patient with her, what would she say?

The truth is, there is a valuable lesson we can learn from Houston traffic about waiting. Traffic teaches us to wait, but marriage requires far more than tolerance. To love your wife, you must cultivate **patience and long-suffering.**

In this chapter, we will discuss how loving your wife as Christ loved the church requires patience and long-suffering. First, we will look at general definitions of patience and long-suffering. Second, we will discuss what the Bible says about patience and long-suffering. Third, we will identify the root of impatience. Lastly, we will explore practical ways to embody the patience and long-suffering of Christ as you strive to love your wife.

Defining Patience and Long-suffering

First, how are patience and long-suffering defined? A general definition of patience in English dictionaries is the act of "bearing provocation, annoyance, misfortune, delay, hardship, pain, etc., with fortitude and calm and without complaint, anger, or the like." Long-suffering is defined as "long and patient endurance of injury, trouble, or provocation."[1] A long-suffering person patiently endures negative (or unfavorable) situations for long periods without complaining. Although patience and long-suffering are often used synonymously, there is one subtle difference. Long-suffering is how one displays patience. Long-suffering cannot exist apart from patience, and it is impossible to display patience without long-suffering. Long-suffering and patience are two sides of the same coin. Now that we have reviewed general definitions of patience and long-suffering, let's examine what the Bible says about these terms.

Second, what does the Bible say about patience and long-suffering? Several words in the English translation of the Bible express the concept of patience. Among them are "forbearance," "long-suffering" (KJV), "slow to anger," "endurance," "tolerance," and "steadfastness."[2] In addition to "long-suffering," these terms are synonyms used in the Bible to refer to patience. "Biblical patience is a God-exercised, or God-given, restraint in the face of opposition or oppression. It is not passivity."[3] But how is the patience and long-suffering of God displayed?

God's Patience and Long-suffering

God's patience is a display of his grace and mercy. God's long-suffering is frequently mentioned in the Bible in conjunction with his grace and mercy. For instance, Exodus 34:6 says, Then the Lord passed by in front of him and proclaimed, "The Lord, the Lord God, compassionate and gracious, slow to anger, and abounding in lovingkindness and truth;"

In Exodus 34:6 and Numbers 14:18, the word for "patience" is translated as "slow to anger."

Numbers 14:18 emphasizes that , "The Lord is slow to anger and abundant in lovingkindness, forgiving iniquity and transgression; but He will by no means clear the guilty, visiting the iniquity of the fathers on the children to the third and the fourth generations.'

The Hebrew word "anger" in Numbers 14:18 means to flare the nostrils, nose, or face. This anger is akin to what an animal exhibits before an attack. Being slow to anger is an expression of patience demonstrated by acts of kindness, goodness, and forgiving the sinful actions of one who deserves punishment. Numbers 14:18 also says that although God is slow to anger (patience), it does not mean that everyone guilty will be exonerated by God from punishment. In other words, patience does not mean "passivity."

Moreover, Psalms 86:16 says, "But You, O Lord, are a God merciful and gracious, Slow to anger and abundant in lovingkindness and truth."

Regarding the distinction between God's patience, grace, and mercy, Arthur Pink says that while patience is closely related to mercy and grace, "Scripture firmly warrants us in affirming some things about one [patience] which could not be about the other."[4]

English Puritan Stephen Charnock distinguished between patience and mercy when he wrote, "Mercy respects the creature as miserable, patience respects the creature as criminal; mercy pities him in his misery, and patience bears with the sin which engendered the misery and is giving birth to more."[5]

The Bible is replete with examples and occasions where God exhibited patience and long-suffering toward his creation. Jesus displayed patience and long-suffering towards sinners all the way to the cross. Patience and long-suffering are Christian virtues commanded in Scripture. Since we can only glorify God by reflecting the image of Christ, then we, as husbands, must love our wives by exhibiting patience and long-suffering. But we cannot display patience and long-suffering towards our wives until we address the root of impatience that sometimes resonates within our hearts.

The Root of Impatience

What is at the root of impatience? What is it that compels a husband to be impatient with his wife? An inflated sense of self-importance and a desire for control are at the root of impatience.

Charnock said,

> "Men who are great in the world are quick in passion and are not so ready to forgive an injury or bear with an offender as one of a meaner rank. It is a want of power over that man's self that makes him do unbecoming things under provocation."

To be "Quick in passion" means expressing a strong, intense desire for something accompanied by a rapid or instant burst of emotions. One who is easily angered is quick in passion. "One of meaner rank" is a military phrase that refers to one being superior to another in rank. Moreover, anger is often driven by desires within a person who wants something that another person possesses, but the other person is unwilling to give it to them. Typically, the reason for wanting what the other person has is not for the benefit of the one who is reluctant to give but for the benefit of the one who desires it. The apostle James identifies the source of sinful anger when he says,

> What is the source of quarrels and conflicts among you? Is not the source your pleasures that wage war in your members? [2] You lust and do not have; so you commit murder. You are envious and cannot obtain, so you fight and quarrel. You do not have because you do not ask. [3] You ask and do not receive, because you ask with wrong motives, so that you may spend it on your pleasures. (Js. 4:1-3)

James says that sinful desires of the heart drive ungodly anger. Sinful anger is also at the root of impatience.

As I asked earlier, how do you respond when you have to wait for your wife? Are you slow to anger, or do you flare your nostrils? Do you respond with loving kindness, or do you reprimand your wife? Do you speak the truth in love, eternalize your anger, or internalize it by keeping silent, or shutting down? The next time you become angry with your wife because you have to wait, ask yourself these questions. "*What do I want from my wife right now that I am not getting? For whose benefit? Is my current attitude towards my wife pleasing to the Lord?*" If your answer to the last question is "no," you must repent and ask the Lord for forgiveness for ungodly anger and for being impatient.

Last, what are some practical ways you can exhibit the patience and long-suffering of Christ as you seek to love your wife? What does love look like practically? In First Corinthians 13:4-7, the apostle Paul wrote,

⁴ Love is patient, love is kind and is not jealous; love does not brag and is not arrogant, does not act unbecomingly; it does not seek its own, is not provoked, does not take into account a wrong suffered, does not rejoice in unrighteousness, but rejoices with the truth; bears all things, believes all things, hopes all things, endures all things.

Patience is the first word that Paul listed in 1 Corinthians 13:4 as an expression of love. As stated in the introduction of the book, patience means waiting or tolerating (long-suffering) another person without becoming angry. It also means putting up with the inconvenience caused by your wife's actions and attitudes. Patience means remaining calm during difficult or potentially irritating situations, circumstances, and events that can provoke anger. If you are going to be patient and long-suffering with your wife, you must learn to endure waiting upon her with a good attitude without complaining or losing your temper. Patience and long-suffering are Christ-like virtues of love that can be demonstrated by your response.

Practical Ways to Show Patience and Long-suffering

How can you practice patience and long-suffering with your wife? The following is a list of practical applications that can help develop patience and exhibit long-suffering.

1. Guard your heart.

Proverbs 4:23, "Above all else, guard your heart, for everything you do flows from it."

Patience and long-suffering begin in your heart. Be mindful of your natural tendencies and sinful desires, which may compel you to display unloving attitudes. Keep these unloving attitudes in check. Watch over the self-centered desires of your heart, and do not allow them to flare up within you.

2. Refrain from complaining.

If you are going to cultivate patience and long-suffering, you must refrain from complaining. Complaining is a catalyst for disunity and breeds contempt in the heart of both the one giving and receiving the complaint.

James 5:9 - Do not complain, brethren, against one another, so that you yourselves may not be judged; behold, the Judge is standing right at the door.

In James 5:9, the word "complaining" means to groan deeply as one who is being squeezed or under pressure by circumstances or a situation. In essence, complaining means grumbling due to an unwillingness to wait or be inconvenienced. Grumbling involves criticism and fault-finding against another. A grumbling and complaining attitude also impedes the development of patience and long-suffering. Refrain from harboring a critical spirit, grumbling, and complaining while waiting for your wife.

3. Exhibit self-control

Patience and long-suffering require you to exhibit self-control. Self-control is one of the Fruits of the Spirit (Gal. 5:23). A man's physical capacities are not the accurate measure of strength. The measure of a man's/husband's strength is his ability to exercise self-control. Self-control is your ability to say "no" to SELF. Self-control is the ability to deny and say "no" to your feelings, anger, thoughts, what you want to say, and what you want to do that violates the Word of God and causes injury to your wife.

Moreover, Scripture says, "Like a city whose walls are broken through, is a person who lacks self-control." (Pr. 25:28) NIV

Proverbs 25:28 says a person with no self-control is a danger to himself and others. A husband who exercises self-control will not allow himself to be ruled by anger, bitterness, or resentment, nor will he destroy his wife with these unloving attitudes. A patient husband is constantly aware of his heart's sinful desires and his propensity to sin, so he proactively keeps his flesh (the sinful desires of this heart) under control or on lockdown as a correctional officer does with prisoners under his watch.

4. Distinguish between personal preferences and sin.

To cultivate patience and long-suffering, you must distinguish between your personal preferences and sin. Preferences refer to a special liking of one thing over another. The word "preference" is sometimes used as a synonym for "opinions" or ideas." Scripture says,

> Do nothing from selfishness or empty conceit, but with humility of mind regard one another as more important than yourselves; [4] do not merely look out for your own personal interests, but also for the interests of others. (Phil. 2:3-4)

Philippians 2:3 instructs us not to be self-centered in our relationships with others for our own gratification. Instead, we should view and value the preferences, thoughts, and opinions of our wives as equally important as our own, even when they differ significantly from ours. Sometimes, your wife's preferences, thoughts, and opinions differ entirely from yours. But to display patience and long-suffering, you must value and view her preferences as just as important as yours. Not only must you value your wife's preferences, but you must also be careful not to label a violation of your personal preference as a sin.

Second, what classifies as sin? The word sin means to miss a mark, to violate what is written in Scripture, or to disobey God's commands. Some Christians, including husbands, tend to make their preferences equal to the standards of God's Word. Paul wrote,

Now these things, brethren, I have figuratively applied to myself and Apollos for your sakes, so that in us you may learn not to exceed what is written, so that no one of you will become arrogant on behalf of one against the other. (1 Cor. 4:6)

Paul is saying that we should not call things sinful that go beyond what is written in Scripture. How does this passage translate to husbands? Sometimes, you and your wife will have opposing views and differences of opinion. There will be occasions when your wife will not do things according to how you believe they should be done. There are times when your wife disagrees with your viewpoint. Your wife's personal preferences will not always align with yours. You cannot label her as wrong or sinful when she does not operate or live according to your preference. Condemning your wife because she violated your preferences stems from arrogance and a sense of superiority. Passing judgment on your wife for something that the Scripture does not specifically declare to be a sin is legalism. If you are going to love your wife by displaying patience and long-suffering, you must distinguish between your personal preferences and sin. Avoid judging her when her preferences do not align with yours. And even if your wife's attitude and actions are sinful, you must continue to love her by extending mercy and grace. First Peter 4:8 says, "Above all, keep fervent in your love for one another, because love covers a multitude of sins."

5. Share your heart.

Patience and long-suffering require that you openly share your heart and concerns with your wife sincerely and gently. In 2 Corinthians 6:11-13, after correcting the believers in Corinth, the apostle Paul expresses deep affection with these words:

> "Corinthians, we have spoken openly to you, and our hearts are wide open. [12] There are no limits to the affection that we feel for you. You are the ones who placed boundaries on your affection for us. [13] But as a fair trade—I'm talking to you like you are children—open your hearts wide too." (CEB).

Paul tells the members of Corinth that he speaks to them from a heart of warm love and compassion, just as a nurturing, loving parent does with their child. Paul models how to speak from a place of love and compassion, much like a nurturing parent addressing a beloved child. Even when love and compassion are not reciprocated.

Has your wife ever hurt you with her words or actions? Are there habits she struggles with or areas where growth is needed? If so, it's essential not to speak "at" your wife with blame or accusation but to speak to her—with vulnerability and love. Speaking "at" your wife can create distance and defensiveness. But speaking "to" your wife invites connection by honestly sharing your heart.

Talking "at" your wife involves blame-shifting and figure-pointing. But when you talk "to" your wife, you share your heart with her. The following statements are examples of sharing your heart with your wife:

- "Here is how it makes me feel when you do or say things like that."

- "Here is what I want, need, or desire from you."

- "I love you, miss you, and need you. I value our relationship and life together."

- "These things that I am about to share with you are important to me because..."

Love your wife by sharing your heart about your concerns and what is important to you. But be mindful that patience and long-suffering require you to speak to your wife from a heart of warm love and compassion. A good way to open the conversation is, "Honey, do you mind if I take a moment to share my heart with you?" If she does not respond well to what you share, do not become angry. But chose another time to continue the conversation and bring closure to the issue.

6. Accept your differences.

Patience and long-suffering are displayed by a willingness to accept differences. Since the foundation of the world, God created men and women to be different. Scripture says,

God created man in His own image, in the image of God He created him; male and female He created them. (Gen. 1:27)

Men and women were created differently by God's divine design. For instance, in what ways are you and your wife different, physically, emotionally, relationally, and mentally? You and your wife are different on many levels. You both think differently. Process information differently. Communicate differently. Have different perspectives on situations, circumstances, and events. You may even socialize differently; you may be an introvert while she is an extrovert, or vice versa. Nonetheless, you and your wife were created to be different. What is ironic about differences is that many couples who file for a divorce do so because of "irreconcilable differences." Yet God intentionally created man and woman to be different. Although God created man and woman, and husband and wife, to be different, He also made the marriage union to reflect His image, as seen in the Godhead (Trinity). God the Father, Son, and Holy Spirit are distinctively different yet function as One.

So, if you and your wife are different by God's design, how do differences become problematic? Problems can arise in your marriage due to a lack of patience and long-suffering, stemming from an unwillingness to accept differences. First Corinthians 12:18-22 says,

> But now God has placed the members, each one of them, in the body, just as He desired. [19] If they were all one member, where would the body be? 20 But now there are many members, but one body. [21] And the eye cannot say to the hand, "I have no need of you"; or again the head to the feet, "I have no need of you." [22] On the contrary, it is much truer that the members of the body which seem to be weaker are necessary;

Like husbands and wives, Scripture commands members of the body of Christ to function as one flesh even though they are different. Functioning as one flesh and accepting differences is also a command for church members, who are the Body of Christ. The concept of functioning as one flesh is also applicable to the marriage union (Ge. 2:23-24).

In 1 Corinthians 12:18, Paul says our differences are by God's design. Yet, because we are different, it does not mean that we do not need one another.

How does 1 Corinthians 12:18-22 relate to your role as a husband as you seek to love your wife by displaying patience and long-suffering? If you are going to exhibit the love of Christ towards your wife through patience and long-suffering, you must learn to accept and appreciate your differences. Just because your wife's gifts, talents, and abilities differ from yours does not mean they are unnecessary. Your wife has weaknesses and strengths, and so do you. As you examine and compare your differences, you will likely discover that your differences complement one another. Some of your strengths are her weaknesses, and some of your weaknesses are her strengths. God knew what he was doing when he created you and your wife to be different. If you are going to love your wife, you must display patience and long-suffering with a willingness to accept your differences.

7. Avoid judging your wife.

Patience and long-suffering require that you avoid judging your wife. James 5:9 says, "Do not complain, brethren, against one another, so that you yourselves may not be judged; behold, the Judge is standing right at the door."

James says complaining is equivalent to passing judgment. The judgment that James is speaking of is not righteous but unrighteous judgment. Unrighteous judgment occurs when you condemn your wife for something that you deem wrong, even when it is not necessarily a sin, according to Scripture. James says the one who acts as a judge towards another will be liable to be judged by the only true and righteous Judge, the Lord Jesus Christ. For instance, the extra time a wife may take to get dressed for an event is not sinful. Being indecisive is not sinful. But if you judge and condemn your wife for these things, you are condemning yourself. How so? Romans 2:1 says, "Therefore you are without excuse, every man of you who passes judgment, for in that you judge another, you condemn yourself; for you who judge practice the same things." (NASB)

Since you have been married, has your wife ever waited for you? Have you ever promised to take her out on a date at a specific time, but were late getting home from work? Have you ever made a decision but later changed your mind? If so, you are disqualified from judging your wife, just like a lawbreaker is disqualified from judging another who is guilty of breaking the same law. A criminal who robbed a bank cannot judge another person for stealing a Snickers candy bar from a gas station. In other words, if you judge and condemn your wife for having to wait, Paul says you are condemning yourself.

Furthermore, James also wrote, "There is only one Lawgiver and Judge, the One who is able to save and to destroy; but who are you who judge your neighbor?" (James 4:12)

8. Be patient and allow your wife time to grow.

Patience and long-suffering are displayed when you are willing to wait for your wife to respond to and make positive changes that result from your compassionate correction. First Thessalonians 5:14 says, "We urge you, brethren, admonish the unruly, encourage the fainthearted, help the weak, be patient with everyone."

In 1 Thessalonians 5:14, "admonish" means to warn, teach, confront, and exhort another out of love and deep concern. This text tells us what we are to do. We are called to admonish. But who are we to admonish? And how should it be done? And how do the biblical principles in 1 Thessalonians 5:14 apply to you as a husband who seeks to exhibit patience and long-suffering in loving your wife?

First, the text says you are to admonish the unruly. Unruly refers to someone who idles, neglects responsibilities, or fails to follow the rules. Has your wife ever been unruly? Does your wife have idle time you believe she should use to be productive? Has she ever neglected some of her wifely or motherly responsibilities? Have you and your wife ever agreed on something, only for her to break the agreement? If so, Scripture says you must admonish, warn, and confront her out of deep love and concern for her.

Second, you are commanded to encourage the fainthearted. The word "encourage" in the original language means to speak kindly, soothingly, to comfort or pacify (Jn. 11:19; 31; 1 Thess. 2:11). "The fainthearted" refers to one who is pessimistic and becomes emotional during difficult situations and may be ready to give up in trying times. Has your wife ever been faith-hearted? Are there times when your wife tends to expect the worst in stressful situations rather than being optimistic? Does she see the glass half empty rather than half full? Does your wife become emotional under pressure? Does she express a sense of hopelessness when you all experience challenging times in your marriage? If so, Scripture says you must encourage your wife by speaking to her kindly, with soothing words of comfort.

Third, First Thessalonians 5:14 says that we must help the weak. In this text, the word "help" means to be devoted to, to hold firmly to, or to support and sustain another who is weaker. When the writer uses the word "weak," he is not referring to one who is physically weak, like an elderly woman who needs help carrying her heavy grocery bags. When Paul uses the term "weak," he is referring to one who is spiritually weak and caught in some sin. Does your wife have any sins that she needs help with? Does she need you to exercise compassionate correction when you are confronting her sin, yet with grace and mercy? Sure, she does. I am sure you would want her to confront you with the same compassionate correction, grace, and mercy when you are caught in your sin. Help your wife. Do not condemn her.

Last, if you are going to love your wife and help her become the woman that God has called her to be, you must admonish her when she is unruly, encourage her when she is fainthearted, and help her when she is weak. Paul says that whether your wife is unruly, fainthearted, or weak, you must use a godly approach that fits each condition. Whether you admonish, encourage, or help your wife, you must exercise each approach with patience. Be patient by allowing her time to grow.

9. Bathe her in the Word and acknowledge her efforts to make changes.

If you want to exhibit patience and long-suffering towards your wife, you must seek to build her up by instructing her in the word, rejoicing in her efforts to make changes, and acknowledging her progress. Ephesians 5:25-26 says, "Husbands, love your wives, just as Christ also loved the church and gave Himself up for her, [26] so that He might sanctify her, having cleansed her by the washing of water with the word,"

Loving your wife requires you to strive to sanctify her by washing her in the Word. The "sanctify" means purifying and making morally clean through the inner working of the Holy Spirit, which transforms the heart. The task of sanctification is impossible apart from God's Word. Since you are called to be the spiritual leader, priest, and shepherd of your home, you must consistently lead her with knowledge of and the practical application of God's Word. So that you can help her grow and become the best woman, mother, and wife that God calls her to be. But washing her in the Word and spiritual growth takes patience and long-suffering. Whatever you teach her from God's Word, you must first apply it to your own life. And when you see evidence of growth in her, you need to acknowledge it verbally. And when she falls short, encourage and build her up. Romans 15:2 says, "Each of us should please our neighbors for their good, to build them up" (NIV).

10. Be long-suffering when she makes mistakes.

After confronting your wife's sin or wrongdoing in a spirit of gentleness, humility, and compassion, you must exercise patience and long-suffering (Gal. 6:1). Galatians 6:2 says, "Bear one another's burdens, and thereby fulfill the law of Christ."

To "bear with" means to sustain, pick up, or carry in the hands or on the shoulder. What are we called to carry? The burden of another. In Galatians 6:2, the word "burden" refers to the trouble and sorrow one experiences, which are the consequences of sinful conduct. You must help your wife carry the load by showing the love, patience, and long-suffering of Christ. Remind your wife of God's unconditional forgiveness available to those who confess and repent (1 Jn. 1:8-9). Remind your wife that we all fall short of the glory of God, yet God is gracious, patient, and long-suffering. In doing so, you are fulfilling the law of Christ. What is the law of Christ? The law of Christ is to love God with all your heart and to love your neighbor (your wife) as you already love yourself (Mat. 22:37-40). When your wife fails or makes a mistake, treat her the way you would want to be treated if you were in her shoes. Be patient and long-suffering with your wife when she has sinned against or wronged you.

As I close this chapter, let me share a story with you.

Rejoice in the Patience of God

When Robert Ingersoll, the famous atheist, was lecturing, he once took out his watch and declared, "I will give God five minutes to strike me dead for the things I have said." The minutes ticked off as he held the watch and waited. In about four-and-a-half minutes, some women began fainting, but nothing happened. When the five minutes were up, Ingersoll put the watch into his pocket. When that incident reached the ears of a certain preacher, Joseph Parker, he asked, "And did the gentleman think he could exhaust the patience of the Eternal God in five minutes?[6]

If God had chosen to exercise his judgment, Robert should have been struck dead before uttering the last syllable of his statement. But praise the Lord today that his patience with us lasts more than five minutes. God's patience and long-suffering are abundant and last a lifetime into eternity. Patience and long-suffering are not only God's nature, but he also displays these gracious attributes as he interacts with his creation.

Conclusion: Christ, Our Perfect Example

In summary, Jesus is the epitome of patience and long-suffering. Jesus endured emotional, spiritual, and physical injury with patience. Christ experienced emotional suffering when his disciples abandoned him, and people mocked him, slapped him, and punched him. He experienced emotional suffering when he felt abandoned by his heavenly Father as he hung on the cross. He cried out in agony, saying, "My God, my God, why has thou forsaken me" (Matt. 27:16). Jesus patiently endured spiritual and physical suffering as he bore the sins of the world on the cross. He did not sin, yet was treated like a criminal. Jesus displayed long-suffering as he endured physical pains, faced hunger and thirst, and willingly allowed himself to be nailed to a rugged cross until death. Jesus exhibited patience and long-suffering by enduring injury for the benefit of the injurer. He endured suffering for sinners like you and me. His death, burial, and resurrection demonstrated the magnitude of his unfailing love towards us.

I want to challenge you to love your wife by dying to yourself. Love your wife by enduring injuries that she may have caused. Reflect the image of Christ by loving your wife with patience and long-suffering.

In the next chapter, we will explore how loving your wife as Christ loved the church — by applying the essentials — is not a human achievement; it requires **divine intervention.**

Reflection Questions

1. In what situations are you most prone to impatience with your wife?

2. How can you better distinguish between your personal preferences and genuine sin in your marriage?

3. What practical step can you take this week to "speak to" your wife in love instead of "speaking at" her?

4. Which of the ten practical applications listed do you most need to begin practicing today?

Chapter 6

Loving Your Wife as Christ Loved the Church Requires Divine Intervention

Why You Need Divine Intervention?

Loving your wife as Christ loved the church requires divine intervention. The indwelling power of the Holy Spirit and the Word of God provide you with the strength that you need to employ the essentials of loving your wife. However, there are erroneous ideas about what it means to be a man that may impede us from relying on divine intervention in our pursuit of fulfilling our role as husbands. Our culture, fathers, grandfathers, and others, including older men whom we looked up to as mentors, have provided advice that initially shaped our thinking about what it means to be a husband or what it means to be a man. Before we can understand how to rely on the power of the Holy Spirit and the Word of God in our attempt to love our wives, we must recognize misconceptions about manhood that may hinder us from being the husbands that God requires us to be.

The World's View of Manhood

What is the world's perspective on being a husband? What were you taught during your youth about what it means to be a man? What is the measure of a man? From a young age, many of us were shaped by cultural, generational, and societal ideals about manhood. We were taught—explicitly or subtly—what it meant to be a "real man." When we got hurt while playing sports or engaging in rough activities, some of us were often told to "shake it off," "be tough," or reminded that "real men don't cry."

Older generations emphasized that a man's primary role was to provide for and protect his family—an idea deeply rooted in human history. Even today, if you ask most men, including those in the church, what their role as a husband is, the most common response remains: "to protect and provide."

Some of us were taught to chase success, make money, and never let anyone control us. Others heard that "a real man is a man's man," someone who leads his household with strength and resolve. Culturally, a "man's man" is often admired—and at times criticized—for standing firm in his convictions. He is seen as someone who defends what he believes is right, a modern-day conqueror or hero. Popular media, especially superhero movies, frequently highlight and glorify this type of masculinity.

Additionally, there are those of us who were told that a man never allows himself to be controlled by anyone or anything. Most of us were told the old saying, "Pull yourself up by your own bootstraps," implying that we must be self-sufficient and not depend on anyone to help us. Traditionally, if a man could not provide for his family, he was considered less than a man, even if he was injured or disabled and unable to work. A man who would not or could not provide for his family is stigmatized as an outcast.

Tragically, many of the ideas we were taught in our youth about what it means to be a man have left lasting and often damaging imprints on our identities, particularly in how we approach marriage. As boys, we were handed ideals that seemed noble on the surface: strength, independence, resilience, provision, and protection. And so, many men step into marriage with a mindset forged by those early lessons—mentally tough, determined to be providers and protectors for their wives and children.

Some men enter marriage with dreams of financial success, envisioning a life filled with comfort and reward—European vacations, Caribbean getaways, trips to the Hawaiian Islands, or relaxing cruises across turquoise waters. The pursuit of pleasure, success, and status quietly becomes the goal.

Others bring into marriage a less visible but deeply rooted desire for control—a need to lead that can sometimes edge into dominance. But perhaps one of the most widespread and quietly destructive beliefs that many men carry into marriage is the idea of self-sufficiency. The self-sufficient husband believes he can navigate the complexities of life and marriage on his own. He views asking for help as a sign of weakness and seeking guidance as unnecessary.

When difficulties arise—as they inevitably do—these men, who believe they are self-sufficient, often resist counsel. "I don't need another man telling me how to run my house," they might say. Or, "We don't need help. We'll figure it out." The refrain is familiar: *"I've got this."*

But this posture of self-reliance often masks fear, pride, or unresolved wounds. Left unchecked, it can slowly erode the foundation of a marriage, brick by brick. The truth is, no man was created to carry the weight of marriage alone. And until we begin to confront the false narratives we've been handed—and replace them with biblical truth—we will continue to struggle in silence, thinking strength means isolation and leadership implies control.

Being a Godly Man and Husband Requires Divine Intervention

The truth is, you will never receive the divine intervention you need to love your wives as Christ loved the church unless you view yourself as God views you. Self-awareness is the first step to acquiring divine intervention through the power of the Holy Spirit and the Word of God, which is essential to loving your wife. However, self-awareness begins with having a proper understanding of God (as discussed in Chapter 1).

Biblical self-awareness is acquired by looking at yourself through the mirror of God's Word, which helps you acknowledge your frailties and imperfections. As we learn to view ourselves through the lens of Scripture, we realize that we are not so tough that we cannot be broken. Scripture says that we are not invincible (2 Chron. 20:12; Jn. 15:5). The Word of God says we are just vapor appearing for a moment and vanishing the next (Jas. 4:14). We are all fragile human beings.

Moreover, our goal in life is not solely about health, wealth, success, and enjoying life's pleasures. Scripture says all these things and the pleasures of this world are passing away (1 Jn. 2:15-17). Solomon, who was the wisest man who ever lived, says that everything in life is vanity (Eccl. 1-12).

Not only are we fragile beings, but we are also not self-sufficient. We cannot journey through life as the Lone Ranger. God created us to be social beings. Genesis 2:18 says that it is not good for man to be alone. In other words, everybody needs somebody sometimes.

Also, we are not the supreme authority. We don't make the rules. God is the supreme authority, judge, and lawgiver (Jas. 4:11-12).

Furthermore, we are not sovereign, with complete control and freedom to do whatever we want. Scripture says that since God is sovereign and in complete control, "who can straighten what he has bent" (Eccl. 7:13-14). Embracing the attributes of God, including God's sovereignty, compels us to acknowledge our powerlessness, imperfections, and inadequacies.

As we see ourselves as God sees us, we also realize our own wretchedness. We are powerless, helpless sinners worthy of death and in need of a savior.

But once we declare faith in Christ as the Son of the living God and profess belief in his death, burial, and resurrection, we are declared righteous and become recipients of the gift of eternal life. The Holy Spirit takes residence in us. The initial step we take in becoming saved, by professing belief in our Lord Jesus, is referred to as "positional sanctification." We become like the Son of God in terms of our relationship with God. That is, professing faith in Christ sets us apart from being citizens of the world, and we become citizens of the kingdom of God. However, God also wants us to be like his Son in practice, which is referred to as "the process of sanctification." The process of sanctification is how God shapes and molds us, over time, into the image of his Son. The process of sanctification is how God uses us to fulfill his purpose for our lives.

What does biblical self-awareness, sanctification, and the Holy Spirit have to do with loving your wife as Christ loved the church? When you examine yourself through Scripture, you realize you are not self-sufficient. You become aware of your imperfections and inadequacies. In sanctification, you become aware of your purpose in life. Your purpose is to glorify God by conforming to the image of his Son (2 Cor. 5:9; Rom. 8:28-29). Conformity to the image of Christ can be summarized as loving God and loving others, specifically your wife. And if you have been married for any length of time, you know firsthand that loving your wife, at times, can be difficult.

What makes loving your wife difficult? Loving your wife as Christ loved the church can be difficult when you attempt to love her apart from divine intervention. You cannot love your wife with mere willpower. You cannot love your wife with positive thinking. You cannot love with material gifts alone because money can't buy love. Loving your wife should not be based on your feelings because feelings cannot be trusted (Jer. 17:9). You must rely on the power of the Holy Spirit.

The Role of the Holy Spirit

Loving your wife as Christ loved the church requires divine intervention. You must depend on the power of God to love your wife. Jesus Christ has given us a Helper to empower us to love our wives. The Holy Spirit, your helper, who took residence within you the moment you believed, is your source of strength to love your wife. The Holy Spirit is the divine intervention you need to love your wife. The following are practical steps for acquiring the divine intervention that is essential to loving your wife.

Practical Steps for Acquiring Divine Intervention

1. Recognize that, despite your failures as a Godly Husband, there is No Condemnation for those in Christ.

Romans 7:21-24, "I find then the principle that evil is present in me, the one who wants to do good. For I joyfully concur with the law of God in the inner man, but I see a different law in the members of my body, waging war against the law of my mind and making me a prisoner of the law of sin which is in my members. Wretched man that I am! Who will set me free from the body of this death?"

Romans 7:20-24 reminds us that there is a constant battle within us to do good, but evil is always present. The motivations for doing good and evil reside in the desires of our hearts. As a Christian husband, you must always be mindful that relentless spiritual battles will continuously occur inside you. Here are a few examples.

There may be times when:

- You want to love your wife, but you are struggling to forgive her.

- You want to be gentle when speaking to her, but you also want to yell.

- You may want to overlook her offense, but also consider punishing her.

- You want to be patient with your wife, but you become angry while waiting.

- You want to speak the truth in love, but keep silent to keep the peace.

- You want to listen to your wife, but you become irritated with her many words.

- You want her help, but you don't want her to give you instructions.

- You want to value her opinion, but you also want to refute it when it doesn't fit your logic.

These are examples of the good and evil that you may struggle with internally as you seek to love your wife. Since you have been married, you may have experienced more success in doing good than evil in loving your wife and overcoming the sinful desires of your flesh. But there may also be times when you fail to do good and instead do evil, even though you are fully aware of what is right. Romans 7:21-25 states that there is a constant struggle within every believer between doing good and doing evil. No matter how badly you have failed, in the past, to love your wife, there is good news. In Romans 7:21-24, the apostle Paul, after confessing his struggles with doing good and evil, goes on to say, but,

> **25** Thanks be to God through Jesus Christ our Lord! So then, on the one hand I myself with my mind am serving the law of God, but on the other, with my flesh the law of sin. **8:1** Therefore there is now no condemnation at all for those who are in Christ Jesus. **2** For the law of the Spirit of life in Christ Jesus has set you free from the law of sin and of death. (Romans 7:25-8:2)

Paul says that although he sometimes struggles with doing good because evil is present, he can rejoice because there is no condemnation in Christ. How does Romans 7:25-8:2 apply to you? It means that no matter how badly you have blown it, given in to your flesh, or failed to love your wife, there is no condemnation for you if you are in Christ Jesus. You can make a fresh start. The indwelling power of the Spirit of Life, the Holy Spirit, gives you the power to live righteously. The Holy Spirit gives you the power to overcome evil and love your wife unconditionally. You might be wondering, "How do I stop holding on to unloving thoughts toward my wife? How can I let go of the hurt from things she's said and done to me in the past?" The Bible says that you should never attempt to overcome evil with evil but overcome evil by doing good (Rom. 12:21). And what good can you do in response to the hurt? You can choose to forgive as Christ has forgiven you.

As I stated, the first step to acquiring divine intervention to love your wife is to recognize that, despite your failures as a godly husband, there is no condemnation for those in Christ. However, acknowledging your struggles and past failures does not mean you should become complacent about your current spiritual state. Acknowledging your failure is a battle cry to take action to achieve victory over your flesh. If you want to love your wife as Christ loved the church, you must acknowledge your shortcomings and declare war against your heart's sinful desires. Giving into the sinful desires of your flesh grieves the Holy Spirit, the very one whom you are commanded to rely on for help.

2. Declare War Against Your Flesh –

1 Cor. 9:24-27, "Do you not know that those who run in a race all run, but only one receives the prize? Run in such a way that you may win. [25] Everyone who competes in the games exercises self-control in all things. They then do it to receive a perishable wreath, but we an imperishable. [26] Therefore I run in such a way, as not without aim; I box in such a way, as not beating the air; [27] but I discipline my body and make it my slave, so that, after I have preached to others, I myself will not be disqualified."

The writer of 1 Corinthians 9:24-27 says that you are in competition and must run your race to win and receive your reward from God. The competitor in the race you are running in is not others. Your competitor is your flesh. As such, you must recognize the battle within your flesh and declare war on the sinful desires of your heart. Like a boxing match, each jab you take against your flesh must be aimed at hitting a specific target. Each blow must be intentional.

The ultimate goal in the fight to love your wife is to exercise self-discipline, subdue the sinful desires of your heart, and make these sinful desires your slave. Self-discipline sometimes requires foregoing your perceived personal rights and liberties for the benefit of your wife. So, if you are going to love your wife, you must rely on the power of the Holy Spirit to help you exercise self-discipline. Self-discipline will require that you crucify the flesh with its sinful passions and desires.

What are some areas in your relationship with your wife where you need self-discipline? Are there any ruling passions and desires that you need to resist? It is not enough to stop doing certain things without implementing a positive replacement. Make a list of unloving thoughts, attitudes, and behaviors that you need to crucify and make every effort to replace those unloving thoughts, attitudes, and behaviors with godly attributes. For instance, if you struggle with anger, cultivate long-suffering. If your fight is against impatience, then put on patience. If you struggle with unforgiveness and bitterness, then work on giving your wife grace and mercy. If you battle with pride, then strive to exhibit humility. Rely on the divine power of the Holy Spirit and utilize fervent prayer to fight your battles. Willpower is not enough. Remember that it is not about your feelings because feelings are an unreliable source of truth and will sometimes mislead you. Your feelings are usually focused on yourself. Prayer and obedience to God's Word, despite your feelings, are the keys to winning your race. You must cry out to the Lord for help to achieve victory in your battles. Remember, Scripture says, "Now those who belong to Christ Jesus have crucified the flesh with its passions and desires" (Gal. 5:24).

The first step to acquiring divine intervention to love your wife is to recognize that, despite your failures as a godly husband, there is no condemnation for those in Christ. The second step to acquiring divine intervention is to exercise self-discipline by declaring war against your flesh. To overcome your flesh, you need ammunition. God's Word and fervent prayer are the Holy Spirit's ammunition to help you achieve victory over unloving attitudes and sinful desires that impede loving your wife. As such, you need to hear, believe, and obey the Word of God by spending time in His Word.

3. Spend Time in God's Word –

Psalms 119:105 says, "Your word is a lamp to my feet And a light to my path."

Psalms 119:105 says two things about God's Word. It says that God's Word is a lamp to your feet, and it is a light to your path. A lamp and light both carry the connotation of illumination. In other words, the psalmist is saying that God's revelation (His Word) is a light that illuminates the path of life that God has set before us so that it can be followed. Not only does the Word of God inform us of His will, but as a light on a path in darkness, it shows us how to see and follow the right and avoid the wrong way.[1] The Holy Spirit allows you to see the path God established for your life and walk that path.

In essence, spending time in God's Word will illuminate your mind and allow you to walk the path that leads to righteousness, which is the pathway to conformity to Christ. A good place to start your study of God's Word is with areas of personal weakness. I recommend you first identify your heart issues (unloving attitudes, thoughts, and behaviors towards God and your wife) and then study Scripture corresponding to each issue. For instance,

- If you struggle with anger, consider studying and meditating on James 1:19-20.

- If you struggle with unforgiveness, consider studying and meditating on Luke 17:3-10.

- If you struggle with passivity, study and meditate on Proverbs 29:25.

- If you struggle with pride, study and meditate on Proverbs 16:18.

- If you struggle with the lack of self-control, study and meditate on Proverbs 25:28.

- If you struggle with overcoming an offense, study and meditate on Luke 6:27-38.

Keep in mind that studying and meditating on God's Word is not enough without application. Recommendations for learning and applying God's Word:

- Study at least one passage that corresponds with each specific heart issue.

- Use a dictionary and define three or more key terms in the text.

- Summarize what the text means in one sentence.

- Commit the passage to memory.

- List five specific ways to apply the text to your life.

- Incorporate the text verbatim into a personalized written prayer asking God to help you apply and live out the principles of the passage in your life as you seek to love your wife as Christ loved the church.

4. Spend Time in Prayer.

> Phil. 4:6-7, Be anxious for nothing, but in everything by prayer and supplication with thanksgiving let your requests be made known to God. [7] And the peace of God, which surpasses all comprehension, will guard your hearts and your minds in Christ Jesus.

Philippians 4:6 says, "Do not worry about anything." The word "worry" in this text means to be broken or shattered on the inside because of a concern about a challenging situation or unmet need. Instead of worrying, the writers say that you are to let your requests be made known to God about every concern and every need through prayer (talking to God) and supplication (to make an earnest plea) with thanksgiving. Why should you be thankful as you pray? You can be thankful, as you pray, when you have complete confidence that God will hear your prayers and work them out for your good. The result of praying with supplication and thanksgiving is a peace of mind that exceeds all human understanding. It is peace, not like the world gives, but peace that comes from Christ. The peace of God, through Christ, will protect your heart and mind, by the power of the Holy Spirit, from being shattered into pieces.

Spend time each day making your requests known to God. Pray for your wife, your marriage, and your children. And last but not least, pray for yourself. Share your heart and concerns with the Lord. And be thankful in advance for what God has done and with an anticipation of what he will do in your life. Walk in peace.

5. Rely on the Power of Christ through the Holy Spirit.
- Rely on the Power of Being in Christ (John 15:1-5).

"I am the true vine, and My Father is the vinedresser. Every branch in Me that does not bear fruit, He takes away; and every branch that bears fruit, He prunes it so that it may bear more fruit. You are already clean because of the word I have spoken to you. Abide in Me, and I in you. As the branch cannot bear fruit of itself unless it abides in the vine, so neither can you unless you abide in Me. I am the vine, you are the branches; he who abides in Me and I in him, he bears much fruit, for apart from Me you can do nothing.

- Rely on and count on the power of the Holy Spirit.

- The Holy Spirit dwells within you (John 14:17)

- The Holy Spirit is our advocate, helper, and teacher.

John 14:26, "But the Helper, the Holy Spirit, whom the Father will send in My name, He will teach you all things, and bring to your remembrance all that I said to you."

- The Holy Spirit is Your Strength. (Eph. 3:16)

Ephesians 3:16 says, "that He would grant you, according to the riches of His glory, to be strengthened with power through His Spirit in the inner man,

- The Holy Spirit will Reprove You. (John 16:8)

- The Holy Spirit will Comfort You. (Acts 9:31)

- The Holy Spirit will Help You in Your Infirmities. (Rom. 8:26)

- The Holy Spirit will Guide You. (John 16:13)

Story: "Rely on Your Father's Strength"

Minister Bob Russell wrote about a father who watched through the kitchen window as his small son attempted to lift a large stone out of his sandbox. The boy was frustrated as he wrestled with the heavy object, unable to get enough leverage to lift it over the side. Finally, the boy gave up and sat down dejectedly on the edge of the sandbox with his head in his hands.

The father went outside and asked, "What's wrong, Son? Can't you lift that rock out?"

"No, sir," the boy said, "I can't do it."

"Have you used all the strength that's available to you?" the father asked.

"Yes, sir," the boy replied.

"No, you haven't," the father said. "You haven't asked me to help you."[2]

Conclusion

If you are going to love your wife, you must rely on the strength of your heavenly Father. You can't do it alone. You need someone bigger and stronger than you. Loving your wife as Christ loved the church requires divine intervention. The indwelling power of the Holy Spirit and the Word of God provide the divine intervention you need to love your wife. Self-awareness is the first step in acquiring divine intervention through the power of the Holy Spirit and the Word of God, which is essential for loving your wife. I invite you to follow the five practical steps for achieving the divine intervention necessary for loving your wife. I pray that as you employ the five practical steps for acquiring divine intervention, they will change your life and strengthen your marriage.

In this section, we have discussed the essentials of loving your wife, including wisdom and understanding, sacrifice and humility, gentleness and mercy, patience and long-suffering, and the need for divine intervention. In the following chapters, we will discuss and celebrate the blessings and rewards of loving your wife.

Reflection Questions

1. Which false views of manhood (strength, control, self-sufficiency) still influence how you approach marriage?

2. In what areas of your marriage have you been trying to love your wife in your own strength instead of relying on the Spirit?

3. Which of the five practical steps (embracing God's forgiveness, declaring war on your flesh, time in the Word, prayer, relying on the Spirit) do you most need to begin practicing today?

4. How can you invite God daily to help you love your wife more like Christ?

PART TWO: THE REWARDS OF LOVING YOUR WIFE

Chapter 7

The Rewards of Loving Your Wife

Being rewarded for hard work is a truly fulfilling experience. Whether it's receiving a bonus, a well-deserved salary increase, or a promotion at work, these acknowledgments serve as powerful affirmations of one's dedication and perseverance. On an academic level, graduating from college with honors, advancing to graduate school, and eventually earning a master's or professional doctoral degree represent significant achievements that reflect years of focused effort and unwavering commitment. Each of these rewards—whether professional, academic, or personal—reinforces the value of staying true to one's goals and putting in the necessary work to achieve them. Ultimately, recognition not only boosts morale but also inspires continued growth and excellence. It always feels good to be rewarded for efforts and faithful commitment towards achieving a specific goal in life.

But as great as these earthly rewards are, there's something greater—eternal rewards. God promises blessings for those who serve faithfully in whatever role He has assigned, especially when that service is done with a heart aimed at pleasing Him. One such role that comes with rich rewards is the call to love your wife. Employing the essentials of loving your wife that are discussed in the previous chapters of this book will result in divine rewards.

Loving your wife isn't just an emotional response or an occasional gesture; it is a divine assignment. And like any godly responsibility, when it is embraced with diligence and devotion, it brings forth both spiritual and practical rewards that far exceed anything this world can offer.

The rewards of earthly achievements are many, but the rewards God gives to those who work to serve, as unto the Lord Jesus Christ, are far greater and more deeply satisfying than any worldly success. The point of this section of the book is to show you that there are great rewards for loving your wife.

Loving Her as for the Lord

What does it mean to love your wife "as for the Lord?" It means your motivation for loving her must be higher than simply trying to keep the peace or win her approval. It means loving her even when she is difficult, even when there is no applause, and even when the emotional return is low. It means your love should not be based on her performance or what your wife gives you in return, but rooted in obedience to God. For instance, Colossians 3:23-24 says,

> Whatever you do, do your work heartily, as for the Lord rather than for men, knowing that from the Lord you will receive the reward of the inheritance.

In Colossians 3, the Apostle Paul discusses key principles of holy living by instructing us to put off the old way of life and walk in the new (vv. 1-11). In Colossians 3:12-4:1, Paul discusses how Christians are to relate to one another, including relationships in general, between husbands and wives, children and parents, and finally, slaves and their masters, and then how masters are to relate to their slaves.

In the context of Colossians 3:23-24, Paul instructs slaves to serve their masters as if serving the Lord. Although slavery has been abolished, the principle of doing one's work as unto the Lord remains applicable to how employees should serve their employers. All Believers are deemed as slaves and servants of Christ. 1 Corinthians 7:22 says, "And remember, if you were a slave when the Lord called you, you are now free in the Lord. And if you were free when the Lord called you, you are now a slave of Christ." (NLT)

If we are all slaves and servants of Christ, as we are, then Christ is our master. Although Colossians 3:23-24 does not explicitly state it, the principle that one should do whatever he does as unto the Lord, our master, applies to every believer, including husbands. Scripture says that all believers, "Whatever you do in word or deed, do all in the name of the Lord Jesus, giving thanks through Him to God the Father." (Col. 3:17)

In essence, whatever we say and do, we must do it as onto the Lord with gratitude. So, as you seek to love your wife, there are a few more principles that you can glean from Colossians 3:24-25 that you must be mindful of as you seek to fulfill your biblical role as a husband.

Love Her Heartily—with Everything You've Got

If you call Jesus Christ your Lord and Savior, He is your master, and you are His servant. So, whatever you do, do it with your whole heart for Him. To do something heartily means to do it with all your heart, mind, strength, and soul. The word "heartily" also includes devotion, determination, and diligence. In modern vernacular, a person heartily devoted to a particular activity is considered a die-hard enthusiast committed to perfecting that activity. For example, I have a friend named Jimmie, who is a die-hard fisherman and fishing guide. In preparation for a fishing trip with his clients, he spends time surveying fishing conditions, such as wind direction, water temperature, tidal movement, and moon phase. There are times when Jimmie will fish alone the day before a scheduled fishing trip to locate where the fish are, in advance, ensuring that his clients have a successful day of fishing. Jimmie fishes heartily with devotion and determination. Tiger Woods is considered by most to be a die-hard golfer. The best in the world. It has been reported that Tiger spends hours before and after a round of golf on the driving range, hitting more golf balls. Most Die-hard golfers spend time practicing on the driving range, pitching, putting, and chipping to improve their golf game. Another example of someone who performs an activity heartily is NBA professional basketball player Kevin Durant. Kevin's practice is rigorous and focused as he seeks to develop his game speed and sharpen his basketball handling skills. Tennis player Serena Williams, Olympic gold medalist Simon Biles, and the Kansas City Chiefs' Super Bowl-winning quarterback Patrick Mahomes are a few others who perform their work heartily. What motivates these celebrity athletes to work so hard? They want to be the best. Another probable motivation for these athletes to perform so well is the reward, such as the gold ring or medal. But it doesn't come easily. Being the best requires one to work hard.

The point is, as you seek to perform the work of loving your wife as Christ loved the church, do so heartily, be devoted to it, and be determined to accomplish your God-given task. Strive, each day, to employ the essentials of loving your wife. Work on, practice, and strive to become better today than yesterday. Work on growing in wisdom and understanding by setting aside time throughout the week to study God's Word. You can also utilize avenues provided by your respective church that help facilitate the study of God's Word.

You can also explore creative ways to express love to your wife through sacrificial giving of your time, talents, and treasure. Consider how you can show your love for your wife by demonstrating humility and serving the Lord with humility, just as Jesus did. For instance, how can you show your wife that you are thankful for her and how much you appreciate having her as your wife? How can you do a better job treating her with gentleness, especially when you feel offended or need to correct her of a wrong, with compassion? How can you work on becoming a better listener when she is talking? What positive and humble adjustments do you need to make in response to her constructive criticism, even when she does not present it in the right tone? Serving her, being quick to admit and accept responsibility for your faults, and a willingness to always forgive are all areas in which you can express humility. Expressing humility takes work, but you can do it. Moreover, work on being gentle and merciful towards your wife. Be patient with her, even if you must wait for her. Work with determination to exhibit long-suffering in tolerating her imperfections and things she does that you may sometimes find annoying. Recognize that your wife is not perfect, and neither are you. You both are a work in progress. Last, as you strive to be devoted to and determined in employing the essentials of loving your wife, always be mindful, day by day, moment by moment, of your need for divine intervention. You and I cannot love our wives as Christ loved the church apart from the power of the Holy Spirit. As I stated in the previous chapter, the war against the sinful desires of the flesh is a daily battle that we must engage in. The Apostle Paul wrote,

> Therefore, I run in such a way as not without aim; I box in such a way as not beating the air; but discipline my body and make it my slave, so that, after I have preached to others, I myself will not be disqualified. (1 Cor. 9:26-27)

In essence, there will be times when the efforts you make at loving your wife will be like stepping into the ring for a boxing match, and your opponent is yourself. Like Paul, every punch you throw must be deliberately aimed at a specific target. The targets you must aim for the knockout punch are areas where you are spiritually weak, strongholds, and sins that are displeasing the Lord.

Furthermore, sin impedes and is a roadblock to love. And it is impossible to combat sin with mere willpower. You need the power of the Holy to help you put off sin and put on the new ways of life, and that new life is the life and character of Christ. Putting on the essentials of loving your wife will require hard work, but the Holy Spirit is your helper and strength who empowers you to do your work heartily and successfully. But remember that you are not working to please yourself.

Heartily loving your wife requires grace-fueled effort, a servant's mindset, and daily dependence on the Holy Spirit. It's not something you can fake. It requires an internal transformation—a renewal of the heart that overflows into your actions.

Love Her Like Christ's Servant, Not an Employee

As you work heartily at loving your wife, you must never forget who you are working for. Loving your wife is not just a job. For instance, a vocational worker applies for a specific job. He may submit his resume to multiple companies, and if a particular company is interested in the applicant, an interview is scheduled. If the employer believes the applicant is a good fit for the position, the job is offered, and if the applicant accepts the position, they are deemed an official employee. The applicant becomes a hired worker and begins to receive wages for the work he performs. If the applicant performs well, there may be an opportunity for advancement over time.

But on the other hand, no one's job is guaranteed as permanent employment. A hired person can also be terminated. As they say in corporate America, "everyone is replaceable."

What does vocation have to do with your work for the Lord? In many ways, modern marriages suffer because husbands adopt a workplace mindset toward their wives. They treat marriage like a contract: "If I do my part, she better do hers." When the emotional paycheck doesn't come in, they withdraw.

The truth is, you did not submit your resume to the Lord. And even if you did, your resume would deem you disqualified. Scripture says that all of our works are as filthy rags (Isa. 64:6). You did not choose God, but God chose you. Even the faith you have to believe is a gift from God (Rom. 12:3). God did not hire you. God purchased you through the blood of Christ. Therefore, you are not an employee of God, but you are his possession. God is your owner and master. Since you belong to God, in Christ, you must do the work to which he has given you to do. As you seek to love your wife, you must always be mindful that it is the Lord Jesus Christ whom you serve. So, don't serve your wife like a man trying to impress a boss. Love her like a man who's already been accepted and entrusted by his master.

You're Not a Wife-Pleaser—You're a God-Pleaser

Let's be honest—most husbands want their wives to be happy. We long for appreciation, affirmation, and affection, including physical intimacy. And while there's nothing wrong with desiring those things, they cannot be our motivation. Colossians 3:23 says, "Do your work heartily, as for the Lord *rather than for men."* We all want our wives to be pleased with us. But the truth is, our wives will not always be pleased. There are times when they fail to give affirmation, respect, or show gratitude for what we do. But your goal is not your wife's happiness. Your motive for loving your wife is not to receive accolades of affirmation and appreciation. Pleasing your wife is a good thing, but it should not be your ambition. You must make it your ambition in the work that you do to glorify God. You can only glorify God by conforming to the image of Christ, as you work to love her as Christ loved the church. It is the Lord whom you serve. Always be mindful that your aim is not merely a happy wife and a happy life—it's a holy marriage. And the way you love your wife reflects how deeply you love Christ.

Your Rewards are Eternal

Colossians 3:24 says, *"Knowing that from the Lord you will receive the reward of the inheritance."* The text says that as you do your work, be mindful that you will receive rewards from the Lord. The rewards you will receive for being devoted to the work in loving your wife as Christ loved the church are invaluable. The rewards that the Lord gives are guaranteed. The phrase "The reward of the inheritance," as stated in Colossians 3:24, refers not only to heavenly rewards but also to the inheritance that you can enjoy while on earth. A reward alone is something that is given. But the text says, *the reward of the inheritance*, meaning that the rewards you receive from the Lord are not of works but of grace, which is God's undeserved, unmerited favor.

Earthly blessings are wonderful, but they are temporary. Eternal rewards, however, never fade. Paul writes, "For we must all appear before the judgment seat of Christ, so that each one may be recompensed for his deeds in the body, according to what he has done, whether good or bad." 2 Corinthians 5:10 (NASB)

God's rewards in Christianity are not primarily about earthly wealth or material possessions, but about spiritual blessings and a deeper connection with God experienced in life. These rewards include hope, love, strength, joy, direction, mercy, forgiveness, peace, and comfort. The rewards God gives are not a maybe—it's a promise. And it's not just about heavenly treasure, though that's certainly included. God's rewards also show up in your life right now.

Solomon wrote, *"He who finds a wife finds a good thing and obtains favor from the Lord."* Proverbs 18:22 (NASB)

When you found your wife, you found a good thing. And you will obtain favor from the Lord if you commit to loving her unconditionally. Be mindful that marriage was never meant to be a burden but a blessing. When you love your wife well, you experience God's favor in practical, everyday ways:

- **Joy in companionship** — a wife who feels cherished will respond with warmth and respect.

- **Strength in unity** — two walking together in harmony can face life's trials with greater resilience.

- **Peace in the home** — love removes tension and replaces it with security and trust.

- **Answered prayers** — Peter warns that mistreating your wife hinders your prayers (1 Peter 3:7). Loving her opens the way for unhindered fellowship with God.

These blessings are not automatic; they flow from obedience. Just as a farmer reaps what he sows, a husband who sows love, patience, and faithfulness will reap joy, peace, and intimacy in his marriage.

Finally, when our life on earth is over, we will all stand before the Lord. On that day, Christ will not ask about your career, wealth, or achievements. He will ask if you loved your wife as He loved the church—sacrificially, faithfully, and unconditionally.

But until then, remember that loving your wife may not earn applause from the world, but it brings eternal reward from Christ. Every act of kindness, every moment of patience, every sacrifice offered in love is seen by Him and will be honored at His judgment seat. This eternal perspective gives purpose to daily choices. It reminds you that every time you love your wife, you are investing in eternity.

Just as one may receive a bonus, a promotion, or academic honors through hard work and perseverance, a husband who faithfully loves and honors his wife reaps profound and lasting rewards. By employing the essentials of love—sacrifice, giving, humility, gentleness, mercy, patience and long-suffering, kindness, and unwavering commitment—you build a relationship rooted in trust and mutual respect. The rewards of glorifying God, including the joy of seeing your wife flourish, the peace of a harmonious home, and the deep emotional and spiritual bond you share, are powerful affirmations of your efforts. Much like reaching professional or academic milestones, the rewards of a strong, loving marriage are not always immediate, but they are deeply satisfying and enduring. When you choose to lead with love, humility, and faithfulness, you will experience the priceless reward of a thriving partnership—a reflection of both your intentional investment and the grace that sustains your marriage union.

But Don't Allow Rewards to Become Your Motive

Remember, the rewards should never become your motive for loving your wife. Yes, rewards can be desirable. But don't serve your wife to get them. The moment rewards become your motive, you're no longer loving—you're bargaining.

God calls you to love your wife sacrificially, consistently, and joyfully—because it reflects His love for you. The rewards are simply a bonus, not benchmarks.

When your motive is to glorify God, you can love your wife even when she doesn't respond perfectly. You can endure seasons of difficulty. You can walk in faith when you feel unseen or unappreciated. Why? Because you're not loving to get—you're loving to *give*.

Conclusion – Final Reflection

Loving your wife as Christ loved the church is a lifelong calling. It requires effort, humility, sacrifice, and—above all—faith in the One who called you to this sacred work.

You will be tempted to quit. You'll face moments of weakness. But take heart—your Savior is with you. The Holy Spirit will strengthen you. And your reward is sure.

When you choose to lead with love, to walk in humility, to serve with joy, and to endure with grace, you reflect Christ. And that reflection is your greatest reward.

In the next chapter, we will explore specific types of rewards in more depth—both spiritual and relational—that husbands can expect when they faithfully employ the essentials of loving their wives as Christ loved the church.

Here is one note for clarity. Rewards and blessings are closely related in the Bible because both are the result of God's favor. Yet there is a subtle difference. Rewards are the result of one's faithfulness, while blessings are freely given. Both rewards and blessings are tokens of God's grace. As such, the terms "rewards" and "blessings" will be used interchangeably throughout the remainder of this book.

Reflection Questions

1. What motivates me most in how I love my wife—God's glory or my desire for affirmation? How can I realign my heart with the right

motive?

2. In what areas of my marriage am I tempted to "coast" rather than love heartily and intentionally? What practical steps can I take this week to re-engage?

3. How do I typically respond when my efforts to love my wife go unnoticed or unappreciated? How does Colossians 3:23-24 challenge or encourage me in those moments?

4. What are some "rewards" I've already experienced from loving my wife in a Christlike way? How has obedience to God's call brought peace, joy, or growth in our relationship?

5. Am I relying on the power of the Holy Spirit to love my wife, or am I trying to do it in my own strength? What spiritual habits can I strengthen to stay connected to God's power daily?

Chapter 8

The Spiritual Rewards of Loving Your Wife

Enjoying the Spiritual Rewards from God

There's nothing quite like the deep, soul-level satisfaction of knowing you've made your parents proud. Whether they were your biological parents or those who lovingly stepped into that role, they poured years into shaping you—teaching, guiding, praying over you, and preparing you to stand on your own. They longed to see you live wisely, walk uprightly, and make a difference in the world. To know you've honored them—that you've lived in a way that brings them joy—is one of life's sweetest rewards.

Most parents light up when they see their children grow into responsible, mature adults. They celebrate your wins, cheer for your progress, and smile at the life you've built. For Christian parents, the greatest joy is to see their children walking closely with the Lord—trusting Christ, raising their families in His ways, and leaving a legacy of faith.

Moreover, there are several other ways in which adult children honor and show appreciation for their parents. Adults honor their parents by showing respect for their parents' wisdom. Adults honor their parents by maintaining open communication with them, not allowing too much time to pass without calling them. Adults also honor their parents by making sure that they are taken care of when they are elderly or ill.

Honoring your parents has great rewards. The lessons learned, good and bad, from your parents are invaluable. The strong relationship that you cultivate with your parents can be precious. Our parents have had a significant influence on the person we have become as adults. We honor our parents by showing that their investment in us did not go to waste. Honoring your parents comes with great rewards.

But as good as these rewards are, they can't compare to the blessings that come from honoring God by loving your wife as Christ loved the church. Your biblical role as husband is a higher calling, a divine assignment, and it comes with rewards that echo into eternity: richer fellowship with God, the blessings of His favor, the power of answered prayer, and a life that flourishes under His hand. Loving your wife God's way isn't just about marriage—it's about unlocking the spiritual rewards only God can give. In this chapter, we will examine a few spiritual rewards that you can enjoy as you seek to fulfill your biblical role of loving your wife according to God's Divine design.

Fellowship with God

Family reunions create an exciting opportunity for fun, good food, and fellowship with those you love. Family reunions are essential because they cultivate family union and strengthen relationships. Reunions allow family members to reminisce and exchange precious memories from the past. Family reunions reinforce and celebrate family traditions. They also create opportunities for family members to provide emotional support to one another. Family reunions produce a sense of belonging, laughter, and joy. They remind us that no matter what we go through in life, no matter how difficult the struggles, family is our most important asset—relationship and fellowship with those we love is invaluable. Although our fellowship with family is essential, no other relationship is greater and more meaningful than our relationship and fellowship with God.

Fellowship with God is a spiritual reward that you will experience as you employ the Christ-like essentials of loving your wife. 1 John 3:23-24 says,

> This is His commandment, that we believe in the name of His Son Jesus Christ, and love one another, just as He commanded us. The one who keeps His commandments abides in Him, and He in him. We know by this that He abides in us, by the Spirit whom He has given us.

1 John 3:23-24 portrays a beautiful picture of our relationship and conditional fellowship with the Lord. While our relationship with God is sealed once we profess faith in Jesus Christ, our fellowship with God is contingent upon obedience to his commandments. The apostle John says that if we keep God's commandment to believe in Jesus Christ and love others, God [the Holy Spirit] will abide in us and we will abide in him. John said, "If we." Then "God." How does 1 John 3:23-24 translate to you as a husband?

If you love your wife as Christ loved the church, you will reap the reward of fellowship with God. The essentials of loving your wife, discussed in the previous chapters of this book, are open expressions of love to God and others, specifically your wife. But how does the apostle John define love? John says that love is demonstrated when you are willing to lay down your life for another (1 Jn 3:16). The thought of laying down one's life is also echoed in Ephesians 5:25 when the apostle Paul says husbands must love their wives as Christ loved the church by laying down their life for their wives.

John also says that love is demonstrated by sacrificially helping those in need (1 Jn 3:17). John summarizes love by saying that love should not be about our words, but must be expressed by our actions that come from our hearts (1 Jn 3:18).

Therefore, if you faithfully and sacrificially love your wife, then God will abide in you and you will abide in God. What does "abide" mean? To abide means to be at home with, to dwell with, and to be present with. Your reward for loving your wife in the presence of the Lord through the Holy Spirit, who takes residence in you. To experience God's presence is to experience joy, fellowship, power, and blessings (Jn 15:11-12, 14; Rom. 8:9).

Like a 24-hour, 7-day-a-week family reunion, being in fellowship with God is where you'll find emotional support, a sense of belonging, joy, and strength. Fellowship with God is a reward for loving your wife. But that's not all. You also find favor with God and receive blessings when you love your wife as Christ loved the church.

Favor with God

God's favor is your reward for loving your wife as Christ. It pleases the Lord when you commit to loving your wife, even if, in doing so, it requires you to suffer unjustly. Peter wrote,

> Servants, be submissive to your masters with all respect, not only to those who are good and gentle, but also to those who are unreasonable. For this finds favor, if for the sake of conscience toward God, a person bears up under sorrows when suffering unjustly. For what credit is there if, when you sin and are harshly treated, you endure it with patience? But if when you do what is right and suffer for it you patiently endure it, this finds favor with God. (**1 Peter 3:18-20**)

Peter says that slaves are to obey their masters, whether their masters are good and gentle or unreasonable. The New American Standard Version of the Bible translates the latter part of First Peter 3:18 as "but also to those who are *unreasonable*." Other versions of the Bible render the word "unreasonable" as "cruel, harsh, forward, crooked, ill-tempered, or bad." But why should slaves obey their masters who are unreasonable, cruel, or harsh? The text says that a person finds favor with God if, being mindful of what God expects, he does what is right even while he is being mistreated.

Peter goes on to say that there is no credit for a person who does what is wrong and gets punished for it. Why, because he gets what he deserves. The word "credit" is where we get our English word "gratuity."

For instance, when most people enjoy a great meal and exceptional customer service at a restaurant, they will leave the service waiter or waitress a tip. Gratuity is a tip, a reward, a favor, and a token of appreciation for the service provider. In essence, Peter is saying that there is no gratuity, reward, or favor from God for doing wrong and getting punished for it. On the other hand, if you do what is right and suffer or get penalized for it, then this, my friend, finds favor with God.

How does suffering for righteousness relate to loving your wife? If you commit to loving your wife even if you have to suffer, this finds favor with God. Your wife will not always show appreciation or give you affirmation. There may be times when your wife says and does some things that hurt or offend you. There may be occasions when your wife may seem unreasonable, cruel, and harsh. Nevertheless, you, being mindful of God, are called to love her unconditionally and commit to fulfilling your biblical role as a husband and obey God's commands.

Why should we love our wives even if we must suffer? We must commit to loving our wives, even if it requires unjust suffering, because we find favor with God. You and I, as husbands, have been called for this purpose. What purpose? To suffer for righteousness. Remember that Christ is our example.

- **1 Peter 2:21 says,** For you have been called for this purpose, since Christ also suffered for you, leaving you an example for you to follow in His steps,

Jesus suffered unjustly. As he suffered, he never retaliated and spoke a harsh word towards his offenders. But instead, as he suffered, he continued to entrust himself to the will of the Father. Why, because this pleased the Father.

You will find favor with God by loving your wife, even if you have to suffer for being faithful to what God has called you to do.

Answered Prayer

Emergency number 911 is one of the most crucial numbers we can dial that provides a direct line to the Public Safety Answering Point (PSAP) for police, fire, and medical emergencies. Imagine having an emergency, whether it's a fire, burglary, or medical emergency, and then calling 911 on your mobile phone, only to get no answer or be directed to voicemail.

Unfortunately, this is what happens to a husband who refuses to love his wife, remain faithful to, and live with her in an understanding way as someone who is easily broken. 1 Peter 3:7 says,

You husbands, in the same way, live with your wives in an understanding way, as with someone weaker, since she is a woman; and show her honor as a fellow heir of the grace of life, so that your prayers will not be hindered.

We already discussed this passage in chapter one, *Loving Like Christ Requires Wisdom and Understanding*. The writer says that husbands need to live with their wives in an understanding way and handle them with care as someone who is easily broken, even if we must suffer to do so (1 Pet. 2:21-24). Here I want to bring your attention to the latter part of First Peter 3:7, which says, *Show her honor as a fellow heir of the grace of life, **so that your prayers will not be hindered***. To be a "fellow heir" means to be related as a brother and sister. Of course, we all fall short of loving, understanding, and treating our wives as our sisters in Christ. We are not perfect. A godly husband acknowledges his failures to love and live with his wife with understanding. Then he confesses his specific sin to God and his wife, seeks forgiveness, and repents. After confession and repentance, his right standing before God is restored. But this verse is speaking to non-repentant husbands who habitually fail at and blatantly refuse to love and live with their wives in an understanding way. The warning in First Peter 3:7 is that the prayers of husbands who obey will be heard, but the prayers of husbands who do not obey will be hindered. The word "hindered" means to strike or cut down, to impede, or to render as fruitless. It does not mean that God will not hear his prayers. It means that God will not answer the prayers of a husband who habitually and intentionally fails to love and live with his wife in an understanding way.

For instance, in the Old Testament, the children of Israel approached the prophet Malachi and asked, in essence, why God was ignoring them. In paraphrasing, they asked Malachi, *We are serving, presenting offerings, and worshiping, but God is not responding. Why Malachi?* In modern-day vernacular, they were asking Malachi, "Hey Malachi, what's up with God!" Malachi answered, "Yet you say, 'For what reason?' Because the Lord has been a witness between you and the wife of your youth, against whom you have dealt treacherously, though she is your companion and your wife by covenant." (Mal. 2:14)

Malachi says, God is not honoring your worship, praise, offerings, and prayers because He has seen how you have *dealt treacherously* with your wife. The word "treacherously" is a verb meaning to perform deliberate, pre-planned acts of deception and betrayal. To act treacherously means to be unfaithful to God and one's wife. In the context of Malachi 2:14, some of the men were unfaithful to their wives because they divorced their wives and married foreigners, as well as worshipped foreign gods. Then, when these men cried out to God in times of trouble and distress, the Lord would not answer. Why, because to commit adultery is to violate a commitment and covenant that one made to God and one's wife.

How does Malachi 2:14 apply to husbands and answered prayer? God will answer your prayers if you are non-repentant and unfaithful to your wife. But a godly husband, through the conviction of the Holy Spirit, acknowledges his unfaithfulness. Then he confesses his specific sin to God and his wife, seeks forgiveness, and repents. After confession and repentance, his right standing before God is restored, and prayerfully, over time, his relationship with his wife is reconciled. Healing from being wounded by an unfaithful spouse takes time because trust has to be re-established and evidence of genuine repentance must be demonstrated by the offender.

Although the thought of God not answering our prayers is disheartening, there is good news that we can celebrate. The good news is that the Lord rewards husbands who love their wives, seek to understand them, and remain faithful. The rewards for a husband who loves his wife are answered prayers.

- Psalm 34:17 says, *"The righteous cry, and the Lord hears, and delivers them out of all their troubles."*

In this text, the Psalmist says, *The righteous cry.* Who are the righteous? The righteous are those whose lives reflect the image of Christ. In essence, when the righteous cry out to God in times of hardship, distress, or trouble, the Lord listens to and hears their prayers. And he will answer. How does God respond to the prayers of the righteous? The rest of Psalm 34:17 says, *And* [God] *delivers them out of all their troubles.*

What an excellent, blessed assurance for husbands who pursue Christlikeness as they strive to love their wives. Knowing that God listens to and hears our prayers, especially during times when we need him most, is an invaluable reward. And even more comforting than knowing that God hears our prayers is his promise to deliver and rescue us in difficult times. And God keeps his promises. Even if the Lord does not deliver us, he will sustain us so that we may endure it (1 Cor. 10:13). Not only is the Lord our deliverer, but he is also our help.

For example. Most people will agree that the most comforting words spoken by the dispatcher on a 911 call, to someone in distress, are "Help is on the way." Help may be on the way because of calling 911, but God is always a present help to those who are his children. Nahum 1:7 says, *"God is our refuge and strength, a very present help in trouble."* We can rejoice that one of the most significant rewards for loving our wives is the assurance of answered prayer. God is our hiding place, source of protection, provisions, and strength, and a present help in times of trouble.

Riches, Honor, and Life

Finally, riches, honor, and life are the rewards of a husband who loves his wife as Christ loved the church.

- Proverbs 22:4 says, *The reward of humility and the fear of the Lord are riches, honor, and life.*

In previous chapters, we discussed how humility, wisdom, and understanding that stem from fearing the Lord are the essentials you need to love your wife. Proverbs 22:4 says that riches, honor, and life are the rewards for walking in humility and in fear of the Lord.

The first reward that the writer of Proverbs 22:4 mentioned is riches. Most of us likely think of money when we think of riches. But what did the writer mean by "riches?" Is he referring to monetary riches or something else? To be rich goes beyond money. To be rich is to be wealthy. If you have more than you need, then you are rich. To be in good health and have a reasonable portion of strength, then you are rich. If you are a person of influence and people look to you for helpful advice and godly counsel, then you are rich. God promises to reward those, including husbands, who walk in humility and the fear of the Lord, with riches.

The second reward that the writer of Proverbs 22:4 mentioned is honor. The word honor here means respect from both God and others. Most church members respect servant leaders who genuinely love the Lord and walk in humility by displaying a heart of compassion in serving and ministering to others. People will honor you as a husband who loves his wife as you display a spirit of humility by putting your wife first above yourself. Church members will honor a husband who genuinely fears the Lord. Other husbands who are struggling in their marriage will sometimes seek wise counsel from a husband who lives by example. Honor and respect from God and others are the rewards of a husband who loves his wife. These are the rewards of a husband who walks in humility and fears the Lord.

Finally, the writer of Proverbs 22:4 mentioned that life is another reward for those who walk in humility and fear of the Lord. The word life here means prosperity, to flourish, to be vigorous, to live well, or to enjoy a peaceful and tranquil life. In other words, the rewards you received for loving in humility and the fear of the Lord are the longevity of life. The life that you can have is like a branch that flourishes in producing vigorous fruit because it remains connected to the vine. Jesus said, "I am the vine; you are the branches. If you remain in me and I in you, you will bear much fruit; apart from me you can do nothing." (John 15:5) The productivity of much fruit in your life is your earthly reward. The life that God gives is also your eternal reward. The most precious rewards are the gift of eternal life and the rewards that God gives to us in glory. We are all recipients of eternal life upon confession of our belief in the person, death, burial, and resurrection of our Lord Jesus Christ. We can't earn salvation. But the heavenly rewards that we will receive from God in glory will be based upon our faithfulness to God while we are on earth. If you love your wife, walk in humility before the Lord, then you will be rewarded with a prosperous life on earth and receive eternal rewards in heaven.

Conclusion

Loving your wife as Christ commands yields profound spiritual rewards. It deepens your fellowship with God, places you under His blessings and favor, gives power to your prayers, and allows you to experience a flourishing life marked by joy, peace, and legacy.

Marriage is more than companionship—it is a sacred calling that touches every area of your spiritual life. How you love your wife directly affects your intimacy with God, your effectiveness in prayer, and the fruitfulness of your home.

To neglect your wife is to diminish these blessings. But to love her faithfully is to step into the fullness of God's reward. Hallelujah to the Lamb of God and thank the Lord for his gracious rewards. But there is more.

As you will see in the next chapter, loving your wife will also result in personal rewards.

Reflection Questions

1. In what ways does loving your wife open the door to deeper fellowship with God, and how does this truth challenge your current walk with Him?

2. How do you typically respond when your wife seems unreasonable or difficult, and what would it look like to love her in a way that still finds favor with God?

3. 1 Peter 3:7 warns that a husband's prayers can be hindered if he fails to honor his wife. How does this truth impact the way you think about prayer and your daily interactions with your wife?

4. The chapter teaches that riches, honor, and life are rewards for walking in humility and fearing the Lord. Which of these rewards do you most desire, and what steps can you take to pursue them in your marriage?

Chapter 9

The Personal Rewards of Loving Your Wife

Loving your wife will result in rewards that are a blessing to yourself, your wife, and your children. Loving your wife as Christ commands is not only an act of obedience—it is also a source of deep personal reward. Many men view love as a duty, a responsibility to fulfill because Scripture requires it. While that is true, what often goes unnoticed is how profoundly this kind of love blesses the husband himself, his wife, and his children. When a man chooses to love his wife with patience, kindness, sacrifice, and faithfulness, he discovers that love is not a one-way gift—it enriches his own heart, his own spirit, and even his outlook on life.

The personal rewards of loving your wife cannot be measured in material terms alone. They are seen in the peace that settles in your home with your wife and children, the joy of knowing you have been faithful to God's design, and the quiet strength that comes from living in harmony with the woman God has given you. A husband who loves his wife well experiences greater intimacy, deeper companionship, and the priceless satisfaction of reflecting Christ's love in the most sacred human relationship.

This chapter explores those rewards—not as distant promises, but as blessings that husbands can experience here and now. They are rewards that transform not only marriages but also the man himself, shaping his character and strengthening his walk with Christ.

The First Reward: To Love Your Wife Is to Love Yourself

A husband who loves his wife loves himself. Ephesians 5:28-29 says,

> So husbands ought also to love their own wives as their own bodies. *He who loves his own wife loves himself*; for no one ever hated his own flesh, but nourishes and cherishes it, just as Christ also does the church,

This text says a husband should love his wife as he already loves, nourishes, and cherishes himself. The concept of "Self-love" in Ephesians 5:28 does not carry the same connotation as how the world defines "Self-love." The world's view of self-love is that one should love oneself without respect to others. One popular psychology phrase used among many, even some Christians, is, "You have to love yourself before you can love others." Or, "You cannot export what you have not imported." But Ephesians 5:29, combats the world's concept of "self-love' when it says, "no one ever hated his own flesh but nourishes and cherishes it." The Word of God alludes to the fact that we all instinctively love ourselves already. And the same way that we love ourselves is the same way we should love our wives. In doing so, we are actually loving ourselves. How so? How can loving your wife equate to loving yourself?

A Story to Illustrate a Point

Imagine for a moment that your right hand and your left hand each had a mind of their own. Each one had its own ideas about life and what was best. Naturally, they didn't always agree.

The right hand cared deeply for the left and always sought its well-being. For example, the right hand insisted they both should be washed regularly to avoid sickness and the spread of germs. The left hand, however, thought that was over-the-top—washing only before meals seemed good enough.

Another time, the right hand warned the left about the danger of touching a hot stove. But the left hand shrugged it off, thinking the right hand was just being too cautious and making a big deal out of nothing.

Here's the part that can easily be missed: even though the two hands may disagree, they are joined to the same body. What harms one, harms the other. What strengthens one, strengthens the other.

So, when the right hand shows love and care for the left, it is, in fact, loving and protecting itself.

In the same way, husband and wife are not two separate lives but one shared life. To love your wife is to love yourself, for whatever you pour into her—whether it is love, kindness, patience, or care—it flows back to you. As Scripture says in Ephesians 5:28: "He who loves his wife loves himself." So, the reward you received when you love your wife is love for yourself.

The Second Reward: The Gift of a Glorious Wife

One of the greatest rewards of loving your wife is seeing her flourish spiritually—watching her grow into the godly woman, wife, and mother God designed her to be. As a husband, you have the privilege and responsibility of nurturing her spiritual journey, and in doing so, you are also nurturing your own.

Paul's words in Ephesians 5:25–27 give us a profound picture:

"Husbands, love your wives, just as Christ also loved the church and gave Himself up for her, *so that He might sanctify her, having cleansed her by the washing of water with the word, that He might present to Himself the church in all her glory, having no spot or wrinkle or any such thing; but that she would be holy and blameless."*

While Paul ultimately points to Christ and His church (Ephesians 5:32), the illustration of marriage gives husbands a practical and powerful model for how to love. Christ's love for His bride is the standard, and it sets the tone for how you are called to love yours.

Christ Sanctifies His Bride

The first thing Paul shows us is that Christ sanctifies His bride. Ephesians 5:26 says, Husbands, love your wives, just as Christ also loved the church and gave Himself up for her, *so that He might sanctify her, having cleansed her by the washing of water with the word."* To "sanctify" means to make holy, to set apart for God's purposes. Think about your own marriage. On your wedding day, when you stood before God and exchanged vows, you and your wife were set apart for one another. That moment wasn't just ceremonial—it was sacred. God Himself marked your union as holy.

Now, as a husband, your love for your wife is meant to reflect Christ's sanctifying love. You do this not by controlling her or forcing spiritual growth, but by gently leading and encouraging her. You sanctify your wife by keeping Christ at the center of your marriage and by bringing the Word of God into your lives together. That might look like praying with her, reading Scripture together, serving together in ministry, or simply speaking God's truth into her life when she needs encouragement.

And here is something beautiful: when you sanctify your wife, you also sanctify yourself. Loving her in this way keeps you rooted in God's Word and shapes you to be more like Christ. In other words, as your wife grows spiritually, you are growing too.

Christ Seeks to Present His Glorious Bride to Himself

The second thing Paul reveals is that Christ prepares the church to be presented to himself as his glorious bride. Ephesians 5:27 says, *that He might present to Himself the church in all her glory, having no spot or wrinkle or any such thing; but that she would be holy and blameless."* Blemishes and spots are the external defilements of the world. Wrinkle signifies internal decay.

The church, as the bride of Christ, is being purified and perfected until the day she stands radiant before Him. That's the same picture Paul paints for a wife who is nourished by God's Word—becoming increasingly holy, increasingly beautiful in the sight of God. A wife who is continuously being washed in the Word is purified of external contaminants of the world, and the internal, polluted, sinful inclinations of her heart. Her heart, thoughts, words, and behavior began to reflect the image of Christ.

The reality is, your wife will never reach complete perfection in this life, and neither will you. We all carry blemishes, spots, and wrinkles—both outward struggles and inward battles. But this is where the encouragement comes in: God does not expect perfection, but He does expect progress. This is what Scripture calls progressive sanctification—the ongoing, step-by-step growth of becoming more like Christ.

As a husband, you have the privilege of coming alongside your wife in this process. By loving her as Christ loves the church, you are helping her grow spiritually. Her faith deepens, her character matures, and her life reflects more and more of Christ's glory.

The Reward of Having a Godly Wife

So, what's the reward? When you sacrificially love your wife in this way, you are rewarded with a godly wife—one whose heart, words, and actions reflect the beauty of Christ. She won't be perfect, but she will be continually growing in holiness, purity, and love for God and others.

And here's something worth pausing on: a godly wife doesn't just love God—she also respects and honors her husband. As she grows spiritually, her love for you deepens, and her willingness to walk with you in partnership strengthens. In loving her well, you are not only nurturing her growth in Christ, but you are also strengthening your own marriage in ways that bring joy, peace, and spiritual richness to your home.

Imagine the joy of having a wife who reflects the glory of God—not flawless, but faithfully growing. Imagine the blessing of sharing a marriage that points both of you closer to Christ. That is the second reward of loving your wife as

Christ loved the church. But there is more. Loving your wife will also result in a blessed home.

The Third Reward: A Home Enriched with Blessings

Where can you find true joy? How can you obtain peace? Material blessings can only produce temporal happiness. Monetary wealth does not equate to happiness. People can be rich but live in misery. But the blessings and happiness that God rewards those who fear him are matchless. Psalms 128:1-4 says,

> How blessed is everyone who fears the LORD, who walks in His ways. 2 When you shall eat of the fruit of your hands, you will be happy and it will be well with you. [3] Your wife shall be like a fruitful vine within your house, Your children like olive plants around your table. [4] Behold, for thus shall the man be blessed who fears the LORD.

The text starts with a profound statement for husbands. It says, "How blessed is everyone who fears the Lord and walks in his ways." The word "blessed," in Psalms 128, 1 means to be fortunate or happy. Essentially, the writer is saying that the one who fears the Lord is fortunate and happy. The word "fear" here does not refer to a dreadful fear. It does not mean to be terrified or horrified by God. Fear, in this text, is a reverential fear; it means to be in awe, amazed, and to respect. It is the fear that compels one to yield to the supreme authority of God and to walk in his ways. To "walk God's ways" means to obey him, to follow alongside, and to imitate.

When you fear the Lord and commit to loving your wife as Christ loves the church, you are walking in his ways. What are the specific rewards for fearing the Lord and reflecting the image of Christ? Blessings and happiness shall be your rewards. First, Psalms 128:2 says the reward will be the enjoyment of the fruit of your labor and your well-being. I do not know about you, but there are times when I like to enjoy a nice, well-marbled USDA Prime Ribeye steak dinner with my wife. Being able to enjoy dinner and commune with your wife is a fantastic reward.

The second reward for fearing the Lord and walking in obedience is a wife who is like a "fruitful vine." The phrase, "fruitful vine," connotes the idea of flourishing in childbirth, or a plant that thrives in producing a multitude of fresh fruit or vegetables. Imagine that your wife is a grapevine that grows vigorously throughout your home, and clusters of delicious grapes are hanging from the ceiling.

What does a wife who is a fruitful vine look like, practically? Your wife becomes like a fruitful vine when she takes care of the home, making sure that everyone is taken care of. She is like a fruitful vine when she cleans the house, does the laundry, goes shopping for supplies, ensures that there is toilet paper in the toilet paper holder, and prepares dinner for you and the children. Your wife becomes like a fruitful wife when she reminds you of things that need attention around the house. Your wife becomes like a fruitful vine; she lies next to you, holds your hand, and gives you a soft, gentle kiss. The blessings of a fruitful wife become your reward for fearing the Lord and loving your wife.

The Fourth Reward: A Legacy of Blessings for Your Children

The third reward for fearing the Lord and walking in obedience to Christ is that your children will be blessed. Psalms 128:3 says, Your children like olive plants around your table. In ancient times, olive plants, the wood, and olive oil were regarded as having great value. The olive wood was used to build furniture, and the oil was used in religious practices such as anointing priests. Olives plants also symbolize prosperity, peace, and divine blessings. Your children are the building blocks of the future. The blessing of fearing and obeying the Lord is an intimate, thriving relationship and fellowship with your children well into their adulthood. The blessings of having a good relationship with your children are signified when the writer says, *your children* will be *like olive plants around your table*. The phrase, "around your table," signifies communion, fellowship, and being connected. And when you are old, aging, and elderly, your children will become a blessing by taking care of you when you have lost the mental or physical ability to take care of and provide for yourself. Not only does God require you to love your wife, but he also commissions you to instruct your children and bring them up in the fear and admonition of the Lord (Eph. 6:4).

Finally, Psalms 128:1-3 is bookended with verse four that says, *Behold, for thus shall the man be blessed who fears the LORD.* Verse four is a restatement of verse one. However, there is one notable difference. The word "Blessed' in verse one is a noun, which means to be in a state, position, or condition of being blessed. The word "Blessed" in verse four is an imperfect verb that involves the past, present, and future. In other words, in Psalms 128:1, the husband who fears the Lord and obeys is positionally blessed. Not only is this husband blessed positionally, but he was blessed in the past. He is blessed with his present, and there are more blessings of God to come in his future.

Are you glad that God will reward you with his divine blessings as you seek to love your wife? I know I am.

If you love your wife, you will be blessed by God. The rewards of God's blessings upon those who fear Him are a promise. Psalms 128:1-4 is a divine Subway sandwich loaded with the rewards and blessings of a husband who fears the Lord and loves his wife by walking in obedience to the likeness of Christ. Not only will God reward you with blessings upon your life, wife, and children. But God will also reward you with answered prayer.

The Fifth Reward: A Home that Withstands Life's Storms

If you live along the Gulf Coast, you've heard the familiar warning: "Hurricane season is here. Are you prepared?" The first part is a statement of fact. From June 1st through November 30th, hurricanes threaten anyone living near the Gulf of Mexico. These storms are not only dangerous but also destructive and deadly. With high-force winds, torrential rains, and flooding, they can topple buildings and erode foundations. At times, they even spawn violent tornadoes that rip through neighborhoods, reducing homes to rubble.

The second part of the warning comes in the form of a question: "Are you prepared?" In other words, do you have what you need to endure the storm?

In March 2020, the entire world faced a storm far greater than any hurricane. COVID-19 swept across nations like a raging tempest, leaving devastation in its path. It claimed over seven million lives worldwide and left countless others paralyzed by fear, anxiety, and isolation. Many people locked themselves inside, afraid to step into the public.

But beyond the tragic loss of life, the virus exposed another crisis: broken homes. During COVID, our biblical counseling ministry was overwhelmed with requests from couples whose marriages had turned into battlegrounds. We received so many pleas for help that some couples had to be placed on waiting lists. A few marriages that were already fragile before the pandemic often did not survive. Why? Because their foundations were weak. COVID didn't create most marital problems—it simply revealed them. It was the viral storm that exposed the cracks already present in unstable foundations.

The truth is, every marriage will face storms. Some couples are in the midst of one right now. Others have just emerged from one. Still others have one on the horizon. The question is not if storms will come, but when and "are you prepared?" Will your marriage withstand the storms?

Jesus answered this question in Matthew 7:24-27 with a story about two builders who encountered the same storm:

"Therefore everyone who hears these words of Mine and acts on them, may be compared to a wise man who built his house on the rock. And the rain fell, and the floods came, and the winds blew and slammed against that house; and yet it did not fall, for it had been founded on the rock. Everyone who hears these words of Mine and does not act on them will be like a foolish man who built his house on the sand. The rain fell, and the floods came, and the winds blew and slammed against that house; and it fell—and great was its fall."

Both builders in Jesus' parable heard His words. Both built houses. Both encountered the same storm. The difference between each builder lay in their foundation. The wise man heard and obeyed Jesus' words and built on rock; the foolish man ignored them and built on sand. When the storm came, the wise man's house stood firm, but the foolish man's house collapsed with him still in it—and he lost everything.

So let me ask you: Is your house built on rock or sand? Jesus calls husbands not only to hear His words but to obey them. He commands us to love, learn, and lead our wives sacrificially. If we obey, our marriages stand on the solid rock of God's Word. No matter how fierce the rain, how high the floodwaters, or how strong the winds, a marriage built on obedience to Christ will endure.

What is your reward for loving your wife? The rock is not simply hearing—it is obedience.

You will encounter storms in marriage. The storms that you will encounter are numerous. Sometimes there will be financial storms. Sometimes there will be conflict. Other times, rebellious teenagers may create a storm. Unresolved conflict can be a storm. Health issues can become storms. The good news is that if you remain obedient to God's command to love your wife as Christ loved the church, you will be rewarded. The reward for a husband who loves his wife as Christ commands is a marriage that withstands life's fiercest storms.

Conclusion

The rewards of loving your wife are both personal and practical:

- You love yourself when you love her.

- You nurture her spiritual growth and grow in faith alongside her.

- You bring blessing and stability to your home.

- You will be a blessing to your children.

- You build a marriage that endures life's storms.

Love your wife as Christ loved the church, and you will not only bless her—you will also reap lasting rewards in your own life, your family, and your walk with God.

Your reward for loving your wife is the divine ability to endure the storms of life.

In the next and final chapter, we will discuss the relational rewards of loving your wife.

Reflection Questions

1. How are you currently encouraging your wife's spiritual growth, and where could you improve?

2. What specific actions can you take this week to bring greater blessing and peace into your home?

3. What storms has your marriage faced, and how did your foundation in Christ affect the outcome?

4. Which of the five rewards in this chapter do you mostly need to focus on right now, and why?

Chapter 10

The Relational Rewards of Loving Your Wife

When Scripture commands husbands to love their wives as Christ loved the church (Eph. 5:25), it is not only calling us to obedience but also promising blessing. Loving your wife produces spiritual and personal rewards, but it also brings relational rewards—gifts that strengthen your marriage and glorify God. These relational rewards include healing, forgiveness, peace, unity, companionship, a cure for loneliness, and lifelong support. First, loving your wife will produce healing and restoration when your marriage seems broken. Second, loving your wife can lead to both receiving and granting forgiveness for past wrongs. The most common problem in troubled marriages is unforgiveness. Third, loving your wife can lead to peace with God and the peace of God. It can also lead to peace between you and your wife. Peace is the byproduct of forgiveness. Fourth, unity and oneness are another reward for loving your wife. Fifth, loving your wife is a cure for loneliness, especially when the children become adults and the nest becomes empty. The final reward for loving your wife as Christ loved the church is mutual lifetime support as you age and your health begins to fade.

Healing and Restoration

First, loving your wife will produce healing and restoration when your marriage seems broken.

- Scripture says, "Above all, keep fervent in your love for one another, because love covers a multitude of sins." (1 Pet. 4:8)

Earlier in 1 Peter 4:1-6, the writer calls us to live according to God's Will rather than giving in to sin. But how can we do this? In 1 Peter 4:8, the writer provides the answer. We live according to God's Will by loving one another fervently and intentionally, because love has the power to cover sins. This love expresses itself through serving, ministering to, and helping others in need. When we love, we do not ignore sin; instead, we bring healing to broken relationships by restoring what is damaged. As we do, we free ourselves to serve—especially those who may have wronged us.

So, how does 1 Peter 4:8 apply to you as a husband? It tells you the benefits of loving your wife. Because love—true, fervent love—covers a multitude of sins.

Let me illustrate the principle of 1 Peter 4:8 with a simple picture. My wife and I share a king-sized bed. Each week, she does the laundry, and together we put clean sheets on the mattress. When the mattress is bare, I notice a few permanent stains that cannot be removed. Yet once we stretch fresh, clean sheets over it and top it with the comforter, those stains disappear from view. The mattress itself hasn't changed—the marks are still there—but it is covered, restored, and renewed in appearance.

In the same way, loving your wife covers the stains of sins and restores the relationship. Love, empowered by Christ, heals wounds and rebuilds trust. It doesn't mean you overlook her sins or pretend they don't exist. Instead, it means you respond with compassionate, gentle correction, clothed in grace and mercy. You love her as the One who knows you, too, are a sinner—and yet God, in His mercy, has loved you. Just as His love covers your sins, your love, flowing from

Him, can cover and restore your marriage. A relational reward for loving your wife is healing and restoration. Loving your wife will also result in forgiveness.

Forgiveness and Reconciliation

Second, loving your wife can lead to both receiving and granting forgiveness for past wrongs. The most common problem in troubled marriages is unforgiveness. However, Scripture teaches that since God has chosen us, we have a corresponding responsibility, among other things, to forgive. As Colossians 3:12-14 declares,

> So, as those who have been chosen of God, holy and beloved, put on a heart of compassion, kindness, humility, gentleness and patience; [13] *bearing with one another, and forgiving each other, whoever has a complaint against anyone; just as the Lord forgave you, so also should you.* [14] Beyond all these things put on love, which is the perfect bond of unity.

As those who are chosen by God, we are obligated to love others, particularly our wives, by exhibiting the Christlike attributes listed in Colossians 3:12-14. The writer begins Colossians 3:13 with the phrase "bearing with one another" and then mentions the need to forgive those we have complaints against, and finally ends the verse with the need to forgive just as Christ forgave us. He is an observation worth noting. The writer mentions the words "forgiving" and "forgave." And sandwiched in between the words synonymous with forgiven is the word "complaints." The word complaint means to find fault, gripe, blame, or accuse someone of an offense committed against you. To complain also means to express (either by one's action or attitude) discontent, regret, resentment, or anger towards another who is guilty of a wrongdoing. Complaints and unforgiveness are two sides to the same coin.

Do you have complaints about your wife? One of the rewards of loving your wife is the ability to grant and give forgiveness. Why should you forgive your wife? Colossians 3:13 teaches us that we forgive our spouse because Christ forgave us of our past, present, and future sins. Forgiveness is rooted in the gospel of Christ and what He did on the cross for our sins. However, our pride and self-righteousness can sometimes impede forgiveness. Pride keeps us from granting forgiveness. Author Ken Sande said,

> As we reflect and rejoice in the gospel of Christ, two things happen. Our pride and defensiveness are stripped away, and we can let go of our delusion of self-righteousness, honestly examine ourselves, and find freedom from guilt and sin by admitting our wrongs.[1]

Sande also said,

> The gospel shows us how important reconciliation is to God, which inspires us to do everything we can to repair any harm we have caused to others and to be reconciled to those we have wronged.

Sande's profound statements emphasize the relationship between the gospel and reconciliation. The gospel reminds us of our need to forgive. Forgiveness is an expression of love that fosters unity, harmony, and reconciliation with your wife. But forgiveness starts with confession. Here is what true confession and requesting forgiveness look like in practice. Sande called this "The 7 A's of Confession," but I refer to them as the 7 A's of forgiveness.[2] These seven principles are based on Proverbs 28:13, Matthew 7:3-5, and 1 John 1:8-9. Sande says that as you confess sin and seek forgiveness, you do the following:

1. **A**DDRESS everyone involved

2. **A**VOID *using* if, but, and maybe

3. **A**DMIT specifically *the offense committed*

4. **A**CKNOWLEDGE the hurt

5. **A**CCEPT the consequences

6. **A**LTER your behavior

7. **A**SK for forgiveness

I have often used the 7 A's of Confession in marriage counseling with couples who have had severe conflict or an argument during the week between sessions. After allowing each spouse to share their version of the conflict, I ask each of them if their response to the conflict was pleasing to God. If their response was not pleasing to God, I asked them to admit where they were wrong in the conflict. After acknowledging their faults, I explained each element of the 7 A's of confession and then illustrated what it looks like in practice. For example, I would share the following or a similar story with the couple during the session. Here is what I would share:

"Let's say, after a heated argument, my voice rose far louder than it ever should have. My wife, hurt and shaken, walked away without a word. She closed the bedroom door behind her and locked it. The silence that followed felt heavier than the argument itself."

"Hours passed, and my frustration gave way to regret. I knew I had to take the first step. Quietly, I went to the bedroom and tapped gently on the door. My voice was softer now, and I asked her to let me in. After a long pause, I heard the lock click, and she slowly opened the door."

"I walked in, sat beside her, and reached for her hand. Looking into her eyes, I said:"

> *Honey, I was wrong to yell at you. I'm ashamed of the words I chose and the way I spoke them. I know I hurt you, and I don't blame you for being upset or for walking away. I'm deeply sorry for what I did. I promise not to speak to you in that way again.*

I'm not perfect, but I am committed to becoming better—for you, for us. All I ask is, will you please forgive me?

After sharing this story with the couple, I ask each spouse to turn and face the other and alternately employ the 7 A's of confession, as I demonstrated, by addressing, avoiding, admitting, acknowledging, accepting, altering, and asking for forgiveness. On some occasions, by the time the second person finishes their confession and asks for forgiveness, the husband and wife are in tears and hugging one another. It warms my heart to see couples admit their faults, confess, request forgiveness, and be reconciled with one another. It is always a tear-jerking experience.

But, as husbands, confession and forgiveness start with us. We should take the initiative in restoring the relationship with our wives when things are broken. We are the head and leader of our wives, and therefore, we should set the example. But you may say, "What if I forgive her, but she is unwilling to forgive me? What then?" This question will be discussed in the next section on finding peace with your wife. Peace is another relational reward for loving your wife.

Peace in the Relationship

Third, loving your wife can lead to peace. Peace is the byproduct of forgiveness. But what do you do when you are willing to forgive your wife, but she is unwilling to forgive you? Some husbands tend to grant forgiveness to their wives only if it is reciprocated, but this mindset is of the world. I address this issue in a chapter on "Loving Your Wife when it Seems It is Not Returned" in my book, "Overcoming the Challenges of Loving Your Wife." But the point is that the world loves those who love them. The world gives to others based on what they get in return. Other husbands become passive by relinquishing leadership and decision-making to their wives to maintain peace. Passivity is fake peace. However, husbands can pursue peace, expecting nothing in return, and without being passive. The writer of Romans 12:18-21 tells us,

If possible, so far as it depends on you, be at peace with all men. [19] Never take your own revenge, beloved, but leave room for the wrath of God, for it is written, "Vengeance is Mine, I will repay," says the Lord. [20] "But if your enemy is hungry, feed him, and if he is thirsty, give him a drink; for in so doing you will heap burning coals on his head." [21] Do not be overcome by evil, but overcome evil with good. (Romans 12:18-21)

In context, Romans 12:16-21 presents a picture of how we are to present our bodies as a living and holy sacrifice to God, an act of worship (Romans 12:1-2). The writer says, "If possible, so far as it depends on you, be at peace with all men." What can a husband do to be at peace with his wife? Romans 12:16-21 provides a formula for making peace with others, particularly with those who oppose us. We will explore the formula for making peace with your wives, even if she is unwilling to forgive, using the practical principles of Romans 12:16-17 and 19-21. To achieve peace with your wife, consider applying the following principles.

1. Bless her if she persecutes you – Pray for her (Romans 12:14)

2. Do not persecute her in return (Romans 12:14)

3. Share in her joys and sorrows. (Rom. 12:15)

4. Show her that you value her as much as you value yourself. (Rom. 12:16)

5. Never repay evil for evil or insult for insult with your wife. (Rom. 12:17)

6. Do what is right with your wife, privately and publicly. (Rom. 12:17)

7. Strive to be a peacemaker with your wife. (Rom. 12:18)

8. Do not retaliate against your wife. (Rom. 12:19a)

9. Realize that you cannot change her, so leave that to God. (Rom. 12:19b)

10. Show her kindness by meeting her needs even if she opposes you. (Rom. 12:20)

As you practice these ten principles, remember that you are doing them as an act of worship to God. You may believe this is too difficult a task. Or you may think that you will have to make significant sacrifices to achieve the peace you want with your wife. You are correct. Remember Romans 12:1 says, "Therefore, I urge you, brothers and sisters, in view of God's mercy, to offer your bodies as a living sacrifice, holy and pleasing to God—this is your true and proper worship." (NIV)

As you implement the principles in Romans 12:14-21, you present your feelings, desires, emotions, rights, and what you believe you deserve as a living sacrifice to God, an act of worship. In essence, you are laying yourself on the altar of self-denial to glorify God and to love your wife as Christ loved the church.

Furthermore, the writer of Romans 12 summarizes these ten principles for presenting yourself as a living sacrifice and how to love those who oppose you in the final verse. In summary of all these things, the writer said, "Do not be overcome by evil, but overcome evil with good." (Rom. 12:21).

So how do you respond if your wife withholds forgiveness? How can you have peace with her? You cannot make your wife forgive you. You cannot make her be at peace with you. But you can be at peace with her by applying these biblical principles that promote peace and by overcoming the obstacles to peace by doing good. God is the One who will hold each of you accountable for your actions. Galatians 6:5 says, "for each one should carry their own load." Sacrificial love and forgiveness can bring about peace and foster unity. Unity is another relational reward for loving your wife.

Unity and Oneness

Fourth, unity and oneness are another relational reward for loving your wife. After listing the Christlike attributes that we should exhibit as those chosen by God, the writer summarizes what he listed in Colossians 3:12-13 with the following words.

> "**Beyond all these things** *put on* love, which is the perfect bond of unity." (Col. 3:14)

Beyond what things? The writer says, beyond putting on a heart of compassion, kindness, humility, gentleness, patience, long suffering, and forgiveness, put on love. All the things that the writer listed in Colossians 3:12-13 are expressions of love. Why should we put on love? We should put on love because love is the perfect bond of unity. Love is a bond. The word bond means to join or bind together. It is similar to how our skeletal structure is bound together. It reminds me of a childhood song we used to sing that goes like this: The *neck bone is connected to the back bone, and the back bone is connected to the tail bone, and the tail bone is connected to the hip bone, and the hip bone is connected to the thigh bone, and so on.* Like our human skeleton, bonding means to be joined together. The word "bond" is also the origin of the English word "adhesive." So, bond means to be connected, joined, bound, and stuck together as one unit.

How do you enjoy the reward of achieving a unit with your wife? Loving your wife as Christ loved the church is the bond of unity. Not only is love the bond that produces unity in your marriage. The bond that love produces is also perfect. Remember that Colossians 3:14 says, "Beyond all these things, put on love, which is the **perfect** bond of unity."

The word "perfect" means complete and fully mature. The reward for loving your wife is the perfect, complete, and mature bond of unity. Unity is the sweet intimacy that a husband and wife can share and enjoy together. You and your wife can experience intimacy on several levels. Unity encapsulates physical, sexual, emotional, mental, and spiritual intimacy. Physical intimacy, such as touching or holding hands. Sexual intimacy is giving yourself to one another to please one another. Emotional unity is being connected to and feeling one another's sorrows and joys. Mental unity is the ability to share your opinions, thoughts, and fears, and to be allowed freedom of expression without being condemned or criticized. Spiritual unity occurs when you and your wife are walking together, seeking to grow more into the image of Christ. Nothing facilitates spiritual growth more than serving together in ministry. Your reward for loving your wife is "the perfect bond of unity." But there is more. A cure for loneliness is another relational reward for loving your wife.

A Cure for Loneliness

Fifth, loving your wife is a cure for loneliness, especially when the children become adults and the nest becomes empty.

- Then the Lord God said, "It is not good for the man to be alone; I will make him a helper suitable for him." (Gen. 2:18)

God said *it is not good for man to be alone.* Can you imagine what it would be like if you were the only person on planet Earth? There was an episode of The Twilight Zone called "A Kind of Stopwatch" about a man who finds a stopwatch that stops time. In the episode, a talkative man named Patrick Thomas McNulty receives a stopwatch from a stranger that allows him to pause the world around him. He uses the device to play pranks and eventually to commit a robbery, but he ultimately breaks the stopwatch, freezing time permanently and leaving him alone. The episode concludes with McNulty descending into insanity. While this episode of Twilight Zone is a fictitious story, it contains a theological truth.

The theological truth is that God did not create man to live alone. Genesis reminds us of this truth that it is not good for man to live alone. The phrase "Not good" means to be incomplete, deficient, unhealthy, or unwholesome.

But God has rewarded you with your wife as your lifelong companion and as a cure for loneliness. She completes you, adequately satisfies your deficiencies, and she is your suitable helper. So, cherish your wife and love her. Love her because at the end of the day, when the children become adults and leave the nest, all you have is one another to share life with, and take care of one another as you grow old together. Your wife is not only a cure for loneliness, but she is also your lifelong support.

Lifelong Support

Moreover, there is no greater reward for loving your wife than the blessing of walking together in mutual support through the later seasons of life, even as age and fading health come your way. You and your wife are your lifetime partners. "Till death do us part" is a common statement used by couples when they exchange wedding vows. The writer of 1Corinthians 13:4-8 lists several characteristics of love. He ends his litany of attributes of love with these words. He says that love,

> [7] *bears all things*, believes all things, hopes all things, *endures all things.* [8] *Love never fails*; but if there are gifts of prophecy, they will be done away; if there are tongues, they will cease; if there is knowledge, it will be done away. (Cor. 13:7-8)

In 1 Corinthians 13:7-8, four lasting rewards of love are worth celebrating. First, it says that love "Bears all things." To "Bear" means to hold up under pressure, or to be watertight and protected from external elements beyond one's control. Loving your wife will enable you to withstand the stresses of life, whether they are internal challenges or external trials. Second, 1 Corinthians 13:7b says love, "Believes all things." To "Believe all things" means to have confidence in or to give others the benefit of the doubt. Loving your wife builds trust and facilitates confidence in one another. Third, 1 Corinthians 13:7c says that love, "Hope all things." To "Hope all things" is to be optimistic about the future. It means trusting in God and staying hopeful, no matter what comes your way. Loving your wife cultivates hope that, no matter what you and your wife are facing, you can remain confident that God has a plan for the good of the marriage and His glory. Fourth, the text says that Love "endures all things." To "endure" means to sustain and stand up under pressure. Loving your wife will sustain the marriage and allow you to stand up under pressure even beyond the point of exhaustion.

Finally, the text says that love "Never fails." The writer of 1 Corinthians 13:8a is saying love will never cease. In essence, he says that love is eternal and transcends the temporal aspects of life. God's love is everlasting to everlasting. Love is permanent. The temporal things of this world will pass away, but not love. Loving your wife can produce a lasting marriage that endures the test of time. God created marriage to be permanent. Loving your wife can last well into eternity. If we do, we can look forward to hearing the voice of the Lord, saying, "Well done, my good and faithful servant."

What is your greatest reward? Listen to what the wisest man who ever lived had to say about your greatest reward in life (apart from Christ). He said,

> "Enjoy life with the woman whom you love all the days of your fleeting life which He has given to you under the sun; *for this is your reward in life* and in your toil in which you have labored under the sun." (Eccl. 9:9)

Solomon, the writer of Ecclesiastes and the wisest man who ever lived, says, Your wife is your greatest reward. So, while you have breath, let your life and your marriage be a living testimony to other couples of the love of God by loving your wife as Christ loved the church. If you employ the essentials, you will enjoy the rewards.

Conclusion

Loving your wife as Christ loved the church is not a duty to be endured but a divine privilege to be embraced. Healing, forgiveness, peace, unity, companionship, and lifelong support are not abstract ideals; they are tangible rewards that flow from obedience to God's Word and from walking in His love. Every act of grace, every moment of patience, every sacrifice made in love sows seeds that will bear fruit in your marriage and in your testimony to the world.

Your wife is not simply your partner in this life—she is your God-given reward, your closest companion, and your greatest earthly blessing. To love her well is to glorify Christ, and to glorify Christ is to find joy and fulfillment in the very design God intended for marriage.

So, let your love be steadfast, sacrificial, and Christ-centered. In doing so, you will not only honor the Lord but also experience the beauty of His promises fulfilled in your home.

Closing Prayer

Heavenly Father,

Thank You for the gift of my wife and the blessing of marriage. Teach me to love her as Christ loved the church—with sacrifice, forgiveness, patience, and grace. Please help me to be a source of healing and peace in our home, to lead with humility, and to pursue unity in every part of our lives. Strengthen our bond so that, in every season, we may walk together in faith, hope, and love. May our marriage reflect Your glory and stand as a testimony of Your unending love.   In Jesus' name, Amen.

Reflection Questions

1. **Healing & Restoration** – In what ways can you actively show love to your wife this week that will bring healing or restoration to an area of tension in your marriage (1 Pet. 4:8)?

2. **Forgiveness & Reconciliation** – Are there any unresolved complaints or offenses you are holding against your wife? How can you take the first step in confession and forgiveness, following Colossians

3:13 and the "7 A's of Confession?"

3. **Peace in the Home** – Romans 12:18 calls us to live peaceably "so far as it depends on you." What sacrifices of pride, rights, or expectations might you need to lay down to cultivate peace with your wife?

4. **Unity & Oneness** – Unity involves intimacy on every level—physical, emotional, mental, and spiritual. Which area of intimacy in your marriage needs the most intentional investment right now, and what is one step you can take toward it?

5. **Lifelong Support** – Looking ahead to the later seasons of life, how can you begin today to build a foundation of trust, hope, and endurance (1 Cor. 13:7-8) that will sustain your marriage through aging and trials?

Conclusion

A Call to Love that Lasts

As you have journeyed through the pages of this book, my hope is that you have come to see that loving your wife is not only a sacred responsibility but also a profound privilege. God has entrusted you with the honor of reflecting Christ's love in the most intimate human relationship on earth. That calling is not easy—it requires humility, patience, forgiveness, and daily sacrifice. But the rewards of obeying God's design are beyond measure: a stronger marriage, a secure wife, a peaceful home, blessed children, and a deeper intimacy with Christ Himself.

The essentials we have studied—wisdom and understanding, sacrificial giving, humility, gentleness and mercy, patience, and longsuffering, and the divine intervention that enables you to love—are not one-time lessons to be checked off a list. They are lifelong practices. They must be nurtured daily, like a flame that needs tending so it will not grow dim. Love that endures is not built in a moment of passion or in a season of happiness; it is forged through trials, strengthened through repentance, and renewed by grace.

The spiritual, personal, and relational rewards that you reap as you seek to employ the essentials of loving your wife are equally lasting. When you love your wife as Christ loved the church, you reap the joy of companionship that endures the storms of life, the blessing of a wife who feels safe to flourish spiritually and emotionally, and the testimony of a marriage that shines as a witness to others. Your marriage becomes more than a private union—it becomes a living sermon to the world about the love of Christ.

Let me encourage you: do not settle for a marriage that merely survives. Strive for one that thrives, grows, and glorifies God. Choose daily to love your wife—not only when it feels easy, but especially when it is difficult. Ask God for strength to persevere. Seek His wisdom in prayer. Lean on His grace when you fail, and rise again with renewed determination.

Marriage is a journey, and like Paul said in Philippians 3:13-14, we must "forget what is behind and strain toward what is ahead, pressing on toward the goal." That goal is not only a successful marriage but a Christ-centered one—where both husband and wife are continually shaped into the likeness of Christ.

So, husband, rise to the call. Love deeply. Forgive freely. Lead humbly. Serve joyfully. And may the legacy of your love echo for generations to come.

A Prayer for Husbands

Heavenly Father,

Thank You for the gift of my wife and the sacred covenant of marriage. Teach me to love her as Christ loves the church—with patience, humility, and sacrifice. Forgive me when I fall short, and give me the grace to rise again in Your strength. Help me to be a faithful husband who leads with gentleness, serves with joy, and cherishes the woman You have entrusted to me. May our marriage bring honor to Your name and reflect the beauty of Christ's love to the world.

In Jesus' name, Amen.

About the Author

D r. Darrell Rose serves as Associate Pastor and Director of Maturity at Good Hope Missionary Baptist Church in Houston, Texas. He holds a Bachelor of Arts in Biblical Counseling from the College of Biblical Studies in Houston, a Master of Arts in Biblical Counseling from The Master's University and Seminary in California, and a Doctor of Ministry with a concentration in Biblical Counseling from Southern Baptist Theological Seminary in Louisville, Kentucky.

A certified biblical counselor and Fellow member of the Association of Certified Biblical Counselors (ACBC), Rose is recognized for his deep commitment to equipping others in gospel-centered care. In 2024, he taught a session on *"Counseling Those Who Grieve After Suicide"* at the ACBC Annual Conference in Fort Worth, Texas, reflecting his dedication to addressing life's most painful challenges with biblical clarity and compassion. Rose has also taught classes on "Counseling Techniques for Restoring Broken Marriage" at the 2025 Baptist Fellowship Association and Power Walk Ministries Leadership Conference hosted by the Noah's Ark Museum in Williamstown, Kentucky.

Dr. Rose is the author of *Overcoming Challenges to Loving Your Wife: Living the Love of Christ*, and co-author—alongside his wife, Cynthia Rose—of *Marriage Without Misery: Moving from Chaos to Conformity in Christ*. Together, they have shared their insights at numerous marriage retreats, pastoral leadership conferences, and counseling workshops across the country.

Dr. Rose and Cynthia are proud parents of two adult sons and joyful grandparents of three. To learn more, visit their website: https://marriagewithoutmisery.comor contact him at drose@goodhope.org.

Endnotes

1. https://www.dictionary.com/browse/sacrifice

2. F. L. Cross and Elizabeth A. Livingstone, eds., The Oxford Dictionary of the Christian Church (Oxford; New York: Oxford University Press, 2005), 1447.

3. Stuart Scott, *From Pride to Humility: A Biblical Perspective* (Bemidji, MN., Focus Pub. 2000), pp. 19-20.

4. Jerry Bridges, The Practice of Godliness (Colorado Springs, CO: Navpress, 1983), 77.

5. F. S. Fitzsimmonds, "Humility," ed. D. R. W. Wood et al., New Bible Dictionary (Leicester, England; Downers Grove, IL: InterVarsity Press, 1996), 491.

6. Thomas Watson, The Godly Man's Picture (Carlisle, PA. The Banner of Truth Trust, 1666), 78.

7. Jerry Bridges, *The Practice of Godliness*, 74.

8. Thomas Watson, *The Godly Man's Picture*, 78.

9. Thomas Watson, *The Godly Man's Picture*, 81.

10. Stuart Scott, *From Pride to Humility*, 23.

11. Walter A. Elwell and Philip Wesley Comfort, Tyndale Bible Dictionary, Tyndale Reference Library (Wheaton, IL: Tyndale House Publishers, 2001), 525

12. Walter A. Elwell and Philip Wesley Comfort, Tyndale Bible Dictionary, Tyndale Reference Library (Wheaton, IL: Tyndale House Publishers, 2001), 882.

13. Elwell and Comfort, *Tyndale Bible Dictionary*, 496.

14. Ronald F. Youngblood, F. F. Bruce, and R. K. Harrison, Thomas Nelson Publishers, eds., *Nelson's New Illustrated Bible Dictionary* (Nashville, TN: Thomas Nelson, Inc., 1995).

15. Ken Sande, *The Peace Maker: A Biblical Guide to Resolving Personal Conflict*, (Grand Rapids, MI: Baker Books, 2005), 209.

16. https://www.dictionary.com/browse/long-suffering , accessed January 1, 2025.

17. Allen C. Myers, The Eerdmans Bible Dictionary (Grand Rapids, MI: Eerdmans, 1987), 800.

18. J. W. L. Hoad, "Patience," ed. D. R. W. Wood et al., New Bible Dictionary (Leicester, England; Downers Grove, IL: InterVarsity Press, 1996), 873.

19. Arthur Pink, "The Attributes of God," 79.

20. Stephen Charnock, "The Existence and Attributes of God" (Kiel, Germany, Alpha Edition Pub. 2021).

21. G. Curtis Jones, 1000 Illustrations for Preaching and Teaching (Nashville, TN: Broadman & Holman Publishers, 1986), 146–147.

22. Jamieson, R., Fausset, A. R., & Brown, D. (1997). "https://ref.ly/logosres/jfbcomm?ref=Bible.Ps119.105&off=5&ctx=+1 19:105%E2%80%93112).%0a105.+~Not+only+does+the+Wo ." (Vol. 1, p. 383). Oak Harbor, WA: Logos Bible Software.

23. Bob Russell, author and preaching minister, Southeast Christian Church, Louisville, Kentucky; submitted by Van Morris, Washington, Kentucky

24. Ken Sande, *The Peace Maker: A Biblical Guide to Resolving Personal Conflict,* (Grand Rapids, MI: Baker Books, 2005), 117.

25. Sande, *The Peace Maker,* 126-132.